A PORTRAIT OF THE SELF AS NATION

A PORTRAIT OF THE SELF AS NATION

New and Selected Poems

MARILYN CHIN

W. W. NORTON & COMPANY
Independent Publishers Since 1923
New York | London

For information about permission to reproduce selections from this book, write to Permissions, W. W. Norton & Company, Inc., 500 Fifth Avenue, New York, NY 10110

For information about special discounts for bulk purchases, please contact W. W. Norton Special Sales at specialsales@wwnorton.com or 800-233-4830

Manufacturing by Quad Graphics Fairfield
Book design by JAM Design
Production manager: Lauren Abbate

Library of Congress Cataloging-in-Publication Data

Names: Chin, Marilyn, author.
Title: A portrait of the self as nation : new and selected poems / Marilyn Chin.
Description: New York : W. W. Norton & Company, [2018]
Identifiers: LCCN 2018028552 | ISBN 9780393652178 (hardcover)
Classification: LCC PS3553.H48975 A6 2018 | DDC 811/.54—dc23
LC record available at https://lccn.loc.gov/2018028552

W. W. Norton & Company, Inc., 500 Fifth Avenue, New York, N.Y. 10110
www.wwnorton.com

W. W. Norton & Company Ltd., 15 Carlisle Street, London W1D 3BS

1 2 3 4 5 6 7 8 9 0

FOR MY STUDENTS

CONTENTS

FROM *Rhapsody in Plain Yellow* (2002)   61

Dao, New Poems   163

I compiled this "best hits" album not as a summing up or a retrospective but as a generous sampling of poems that, thus far, could represent my personal practice and trajectory as a poet. I have organized this collection loosely in chronological order, starting from my first book, *Dwarf Bamboo*, which I wrote in my twenties, and continuing to the present with the dire warning of "Peony Apocalypse." I am happy to include poems that have been widely anthologized and that students and teachers have often shared. I believe that an activist poet must write poems the world can appreciate on many levels. My early identity and love poems were influenced by the imagism of Ezra Pound and William Carlos Williams. Trusting to the clarity of the object, I composed the line according to the clear phrasing of my own Toisanese-American cadence instead of metronomically. Many poems in my second book, *The Phoenix Gone, the Terrace Empty*— "How I Got That Name," "Turtle Soup," and "The Floral Apron"— have been student favorites. "Autumn Leaves" was widely exhibited on the MTA for a time. I am gratified that some of my poems have served the people for decades. From the start of my career I waxed personal and political and have sought to be an activist-subversive-radical-immigrant-feminist-transnational-Buddhist-neoclassical-nerd poet who was always on her soapbox with a bag of tricks.

I see myself as an inventor of a fusionist aesthetics, of bilingual and bicultural hybrid forms. For decades I have been toying with the Chinese-American quatrain, stringing beautiful and subversive jewels into fractured necklaces. I also created a thing called Sonnetnese where the Chinese lyric and the sonnet merge together, sometimes magically, sometimes fitfully. Included are reimagined blues poems, ballads, folk songs, and bad-girl haiku that offer social and political critique sometimes blatantly, sometimes masked with subtle musicality. Inspired by a wide range of ideas from East and West, from antiquity to modernity, I considered each poem as an active canvas, where the cross-fertilization of myriad styles and ideas could collide in meaningful ways. For readers who like more difficult and experimental work, I have selected a few longer digressive jazzy pieces, such as the eponymous "Rhapsody in Plain Yellow" and "A Portrait of the Self as Nation," that meander joyfully like jazz compositions but fulfill their intention and purpose upon returning to their original themes.

A small group of translations are meant to remind the reader that I began as a precocious reader and translator of poetry. My early ambition was to become a polyglot poet able to read poetry in at least ten languages, though I soon realized that life was too short for such impossible endeavors.

I have also chosen a fistful of prose-poems, *haibun,* and manifestos. These hybrid experiments untethered my bolder surreal imagination and are a bridge to the weird subversive fiction in *Revenge of the Mooncake Vixen.*

Finally, two sections of new poems are included to dramatize my satirical palette. Their auspicious presence is a promise to my readers that this wild-girl poet is engaged in perpetual renewal and that there is more raucous work to come.

ACKNOWLEDGMENTS

It is difficult for a poet to choose among her lovely children. I had solicited several poets and friends for their keen advice. I thank Bob Grunst, my lucky charm, who has been my faithful first reader for many years. Floyd Cheung, a brilliant anthologizer and teacher, with a keen eye and generous heart, gave me great insight into the role of poetry in the classroom, and my dear old friend Kate Sontag read enthusiastically with a fine-tooth comb. I thank my beloved surrogate mother, Dorothea Kehler, for her meticulous eye, and Professor Alvin Cohen for his enduring advice on ancient Chinese matters. For her continuous love and support, I thank my editor extraordinaire and sister writer, Jill Bialosky, who fights valiantly for poetry and poets, and I thank the W. W. Norton family that keeps the magical engine going. And, of course, I thank Sandy Djkstra, who dares to represent this aging girl poet; and I thank all the hardworking sisters at the Sandra Djkstra Agency, with a special shout-out to Elise Capron and Andrea Cavallero. I thank Walter K for his love and encouragement.

It is impossible to mention all the people and arts and literary agencies and foundations that have supported my work throughout my longish, productive career. These poems could not have flourished without their compassion and generosity. I hope that I have thanked them properly in my other books.

Specifically, for the workings of this project, I would like to thank Joseph Bruchac, who had the courage to publish my first book, *Dwarf Bamboo*, under the iconic Greenfield Review Press imprint in 1995. I thank Milkweed Editions for bringing out two editions of *The Phoenix Gone, the Terrace Empty* (1994, 2009). I thank Emilie Buchwald, Daniel Slager, and the subsequent editors and staff for keeping the bird alive. "Snow Falls on China's Land," my translation of Ai Qing's famous poem, was collected in *The Selected Poems of Ai Qing*, edited by Eugene Eoyang, Indiana University Press, in association with Foreign Languages Press (1982). I thank the International Writing Program at the University of Iowa for giving me the opportunity to translate both Ai Qing and Gozo Yoshimasu. My co-translation of Gozo's "A,D,R,E,N,A,L,I,N" was first published in *Devil's Wind: A Thousand Steps or More*, edited by Thomas Fitzsimmons, Oakland University Press (1980). "Bamboo, the Dance" was written for the Terezin Music Foundation and was collected in *Liberation*, edited by Mark Ludwig, Beacon Press (2015).

In regard to more recent work, I am grateful to the editors of the following journals where individual poems were published:

Catamaran: "Scary Poem"
Lana Turner: "Brown Girl Manifesto, One of Many"
The Massachusetts Review: "Immigrant Dream," "Chaos Had No Eyes"
The Offing: "For Mitsuye Yamada on Her 90th Birthday"
Poem-a-Day/the Academy of American Poets: "Peony Apocalypse"
Poetry: "Little Box Opens Up" and for my translations of Ho Xuan Huong's "Floating Sweet Dumpling," "Jackfruit," "Lamenting Widow," "Snail," and "Wasps"
Prairie Schooner: "Thanksgiving at the Brewsters," "Dead Buddha," "First Duck," "Dogdom," and "Indigestion"

A PORTRAIT OF THE SELF AS NATION

FROM
DWARF BAMBOO (1987)

I do not say that their roots are still weak;
I do not say that their shade is still small.

—BAI JUYI (around 805),
"Planting Bamboo"

THE END OF A BEGINNING

The beginning is always difficult.
The immigrant worked his knuckles to the bone
only to die under the wheels of the railroad.
One thousand years before him, his ancestor fell
building yet another annex to the Great Wall—
and was entombed within his work. And I,
the beginning of an end, the end of a beginning,
sit here, drink unfermented green tea,
scrawl these paltry lines for you. Grandfather,
on your one-hundredth birthday, I have
the answers to your last riddles:

This is why the baboon's ass is red.
Why horses lie down only in moments of disaster.
Why the hyena's back is forever scarred.
Why, that one hare who was saved, splits his upper lip,
in a fit of hysterical laughter.

WE ARE A YOUNG NATION, UNCLE

Old river, once blue-mercurial—
Now lackluster and pale as balm;
The forests and dark alcoves
I remember once
Echoed with tall battles,
Are now driven to the remains of peace:
Burnt fields, dead tallow,
Dry brown dregs of a newborn earth.
We are a young nation, uncle.
Though you keep clutching
Your heart, squawking and honking,
For the old gargoyle, death
Has pressed her body tautly over yours.
We fought the best we could:
Boiled five fingers of ginseng,
Burnt paper coins,
Chanted the Gao Wang Sutra.
But dying men need no money;
What you conquered
Will be divided later—
When your name, that one distinct syllable,
Walks out the door;
When your daughter marries
Into the next village,
Dragging with her
Your last good hen
For the New Year's sacrifice.
Old man, beware,
Ling Ling is marrying a general;
Her pelvis may be ruined
For ten thousand years.

UNTRIMMED MOURNING

The mourning gown
is an untrimmed sack,
fillets of female
nettle hemp.

I supped congee twice
a day, gulped down
this loneliness
for ten years, loyal.

The dead landlord
still whips his wife—
she wails for a century
and a half.

But the poor man
has no servants,
only small pink babies
and one good hog.

Soon, I'll drag her to market
by her short hind legs—
"Rich man, have you no
dollars to taste?"

THE CRICKET

I am sad for the cricket,
Sadder for the late
First century B.C. Tibetans
Who tried to get rid of it.

Billions of yellow-black
Herbivorous villains
Devoured the Himalayan Valley,
Now as good as the Dead Sea,

Moved prodigiously over
The Yangtze, desecrated
The shrine of the Gods
Of Fruition and Harvest.

A cricket can be a friend.
As individuals they're all right.
Before her exile, Yang Guifei
Held one in her palm.

No wonder the Grand Eunuch
Of the Dowager Cixi said
Unleash it and it will kill;
Cage it, it will sing.

AFTER MY LAST PAYCHECK FROM THE FACTORY, TWO THIN COUPONS, FOUR TIN DOLLARS, I INVITED OLD LIU FOR AN AFTERNOON MEAL

for the Chinese Cultural Revolution
and all that was wrong with my life

I ordered vegetables and he ordered dog,
the cheapest kind, mushu, but without the cakes.
I watched him smack his greasy lips
and thought of home, my lover's gentle kisses—
his faint aroma, still with me now.

I confided with a grief too real,
"This is not what I expected"
and bit my lip to keep from crying,
"I've seen enough, I want to go home."
But, suddenly, I was seized by a vision

reminding me why I had come: two girls
in uniform, red bandanas and armbands
shouting slogans and Maoist songs,
"the East is red, the sun is rising";
promises of freedom and a better world.

Trailing them was their mascot of Youth,
a creature out of Dr. Seuss or Lewis Carroll,
purplish pink, variegated and prancing.
I stood in awe of its godlike beauty
until the realist Liu disrupted my mirage.

"It's the dog I ordered and am eating still!"
he mumbled with a mouthful of wine.
And as it came closer I saw the truth:
its spots were not of breeding or exotic import,
but rampant colonies of scabies and fleas,

which, especially red in its forbidden country,
blazed a trail through the back of its woods;
and then, its forehead bled with worms,
so many and complex as if *they* did its thinking.
I rubbed my eyes, readjusted the world . . .

Then focused back on his gruesome dish
trimmed with parsley and rinds of orange.
One piece of bone, unidentified which,
stared at me like a goat's pleading eye
or the shiny new dollar I'd just lost.

Old Liu laughed and slapped my back,
"You American Chinese are hard to please."
Then, stuck his filthy chopsticks into my sauce.
"Mmmm, seasoning from Beijing, the best
since opium," then, pointed to a man

sitting behind me, a stout provincial governor
who didn't have to pay after eating the finest
Chinese pug, twenty-five yuan a leg.
He picked his teeth with a splintered shin,
Burped and farted, flaunting his wealth.

Old Liu said with wine breath to kill,
"My cousin, don't be disillusioned,
his pride will be molested, his dignity violated,
and he as dead as the four-legged he ate
two short kilometers before home."

WE ARE AMERICANS NOW, WE LIVE
IN THE TUNDRA

Today in hazy San Francisco, I face seaward
Toward China, a giant begonia—

Pink, fragrant, bitten
By verdigris and insects. I sing her

A blues song; even a Chinese girl gets the blues,
Her reticence is black and blue.

Let's sing about the extinct
Bengal tigers, about giant Pandas—

"Ling Ling loves Xing Xing . . . yet,
We will not mate. We are

Not impotent, we are important.
We blame the environment, we blame the zoo!"

What shall we plant for the future?
Bamboo, sassafras, coconut palms? No!

Legumes, wheat, maize, old swine
To milk the new.

We are Americans now, we live in the tundra
Of the logical, a sea of cities, a wood of cars.

Farewell my ancestors:
Hirsute Taoists, failed scholars, farewell

My wetnurse who feared and loathed the Catholics,
Who called out

> Now that half-men have occupied Canton
> Hide your daughters, lock your doors!

A CHINAMAN'S CHANCE

If you were a Chinese born in America, who would you believe
Plato who said what Socrates said
Or Confucius in his bawdy way:
              "So a male child is born to you
              I am happy, very very happy."

▪

The railroad killed your great-grandfather.
His arms here, his legs there,
How can we remake ourselves in his image?

Your father worked his knuckles black,
So you might have pink cheeks. Your father
Burped you on the back; why must you water his face?

Your father was happy, he was charred by the sun,
Danced and sang until he died at twenty-one.

Lord, don't you like my drinking. Even Jesus
Had a few in his day with Mary before
He gambled his life for us on the cross—

And for us he lost his life, for us.

Your body is growing, changing, running
Away from your soul. Look,

Not a sun but a gold coin at the horizon,
Chase after it, my friend, after it.

▪

Why does the earth move backward
As we walk ahead? Why does mother's
Blood stain this hand-me-down shirt?

This brown of old tea, the yellow ring
Around the same porcelain cup. They stayed

Stone-faced as paired lions, prepared
As nightwatch at the frontier gate.

We have come small and wooden, tanned brown
As oak pillars, eyes peering straight
Through vinyl baggage and uprooted shoes.

We shall gather their leftovers: jimson and velvets,
Crocuses that have burst-bloomed through walks.
We shall shatter this ancient marble, veined and glorious . . .

Little path, golden arrows, won't you pave
My future in another child's neighborhood?

Night: black starred canopy, piece
Of Chinese silk, dank with must and cedar,
Pulled down from the source, a cardboard bolt.

FIRST LESSONS
(dedicated to the character 好 or "goodness")

1.

I got up; a red shiner bloomed
like a rose in my eye. She said,
"A present fit for a queen . . .served
by the hand that fed you, soothed you
and presently, slaps you to your senses.

"Your goddess of Mercy has spoken."

She ran, blonde hair ablaze,
dust settling on asphalt.

I did it again.
I got up from the blood and the mud
crying like a bullcalf,
not for the wound but for the dress.

2.

This is how I remember *goodness.*

A woman whose lipstick smells of lilac leans over a child.
She says, "Have you been good?"
The child, kneels like a supplicant,
looks up, whispers, "always."

3.

Dust we are made, dust we leave behind—
The dress shall be clean no matter the circumstance.
My friend, my foe, wearing worn Levis and a T-shirt,
Hides in the schoolyard, now, with her black Labrador.

4.

I learned *goodness* before I learned my name.
I learned the strokes, their order, but never the message:

that the good shall never rise from their knees is my
river-to-cross.

ODE TO ANGER

Soak in a hot bath;
arrange my futuristic hair,
then, the futon & the cushioned tatami.
Cut orchids, cut fruit.
Set the table for plenty
(but there is only one of me).
And here you come—
a cricket's dance in the woods—
in a fog-colored zoot suit.
Your eyes are red & bleary.
I am practicing *good purity*.
I do not get angry.

But here comes my father with the tiger's claw.
He paces and frets; I get no rest.
The caged animal must be released.

Here comes my mother with the serpent's touch.
I know the *dim mak:* the touch of death,
I know the softness of the temples,
the groin, the heart.

Here come my sisters with the lizard's tongue
to expel the secret in a moment's hiss.
But they are slow on their haunches.
I shall strike first.

The weir-basket was a snare;
the fish within were dying.
You promised me fresh fish.
You promised unconditional love and providence.

But here comes my brother with the ox's heart
to explain the world in a plum's pit.
He is not your kind.
You don't understand his plight;
nor does he your fomenting silence.

Tiger's claw, serpent's touch, lizard's tongue, ox's heart.
The caged animal is released.
I believe in the touch of life.
I shall keep my secret always.
Although you have lost your way,
you have never forsaken me.
you have been whole.
you have been good.

REPULSE BAY
Hong Kong, Summer 1980

1.

Washed ashore
At Repulse Bay
Creatures that outgrew their shells—
I saw a mussel hang
On a shell's hinge: the sun
Turned its left side brown
What remained tarried
Around the lips
Like human tongue
Unfit for speech

Suddenly, the sea
Sweeps it up, with
A stub-necked bottle, bits of feces and the news
Printed in red and black
Bilingual editions for the Colonialists
And two-bit Japanese tourists
Seeking thrills

2.

Back to Kowloon, in Granny's
One room apartment, her laundry waves
On her sun-filled balcony—
I recognize some of mine: blue jeans, bright T's
A black lace bra on a hook . . .
Two stories below, an old hawker
Selling abalone on a stick, chicken asses
Pig ears, tripe of all species burnt pink—
Looks up, shakes his fist

3.

The rain over Hong Kong falls
Over all of us, Mei Ling, though
This postcard will tell you nothing
About the country I have lost

Overhead, a building blinks
Of Rolex, Omega and yet
Another brand that ticks

4.

Last night, drunk out of my mind
I promised everybody visas and a good time
(should they make it to America)
Autumn is here now, though
There are no rustling New England leaves
Or Oregon grapes tugging the vines

5.

How the sun shines through the monsoon brightly
On the small men selling viscera
On the dead and swimming creatures of the sea

TWO POEMS FOR MIEKO

UNREQUITED LOVE

Because you stared into the black lakes of her eyes,
you shall drown in them.

Because you tasted the persimmon on her lips,
you shall dig your moist grave.

Her rope of black hair does not signify a ladder of escape,
but of capture,

the warm flesh of her arms and thighs—not cradles of comfort,
but of despair.

She shall always be waiting for you in an empty room
overlooking the sea.

She shall always sit this way, her back toward you,
her shoulders bare,

her silk kimono in manifolds around her waist—
blue as the changeless sea.

You sit prostrate before her, bruise your forehead,
chant the Dharmas.

Five thousand years together in the same four-and-a-half-mat
   room,
And she has not learned to love you.

LOVE POEM FROM NAGASAKI

To say you are beautiful, to say
trees are, grass is, everything under
the weather—you are not really, no.

But the dark cloud exposing a rim of sun,
the river sedge dotted with strange new flowers,
ten thousand dragonflies spinning around the moon . . .

Suddenly, the earth emits a fragrance
deadlier than the teeming of flowers.
Tonight I am in love—
            from the squat houses of Nagasaki,

doves, bats, gnats
fly out
ecumenically.

THE PHOENIX GONE, THE TERRACE EMPTY (1994)

ALTAR

I tell her she has outlived her usefulness.
I point to the corner where dust gathers,
where light has never touched. But there she sits,
a thousand years, hands folded, in a tattered armchair,
with yesterday's news, "The Golden Mountain Edition."
The morning sun slants down the broken eaves,
shading half of her sallow face.

On the upper northwest corner (I'd consulted a geomancer),
a deathtrap shines on the dying bougainvillea.
The carcass of a goatmoth hangs upside-down,
hollowed out. The only evidence
of her seasonal life is a dash
of shimmery powder, a last cry.

She, who was attracted to that bare bulb,
who danced around that immigrant dream,
will find her end here, this corner,
this solemn altar.

THE BARBARIANS ARE COMING

War chariots thunder, horses neigh, *the barbarians are coming*.

What are we waiting for, young nubile women pointing at the wall,
the barbarians are coming.

They have heard about a weakened link in the wall. *So, the barbarians
have ears among us*.

So deceive yourself with illusions: you are only one woman, holding one
broken brick in the wall.

So deceive yourself with illusions: as if you matter, that brick and that
wall.

The barbarians are coming: they have red beards or beardless with a top
knot.

The barbarians are coming: they are your fathers, brothers, teachers, lovers;
and they are clearly an other.

The barbarians are coming:

> If you call me a horse, I must be a horse.
> If you call me a bison, I am equally guilty.

When a thing is true and is correctly described, one doubles the blame by
not admitting it: so, Zhuangzi, himself, was a barbarian king!

Horse, horse, bison, bison, *the barbarians are coming*—

and how they love to come.

The smells of the great frontier exult in them.

HOW I GOT THAT NAME
an essay on assimilation

I am Marilyn Mei Ling Chin.
Oh, how I love the resoluteness
of that first person singular
followed by that stalwart indicative
of "be," without the uncertain i-n-g
of "becoming." Of course,
the name had been changed
somewhere between Angel Island and the sea,
when my father the paperson
in the late 1950s
obsessed with a bombshell blonde
transliterated "Mei Ling" to "Marilyn."
And nobody dared question
his initial impulse—for we all know
lust drove men to greatness,
not goodness, not decency.
And there I was, a wayward pink baby,
named after some tragic white woman
swollen with gin and Nembutal.
My mother couldn't pronounce the "r."
She dubbed me "Numba one female offshoot"
for brevity: henceforth, she will live and die
in sublime ignorance, flanked
by loving children and the "kitchen deity."
While my father dithers,
a tomcat in Hong Kong trash—
a gambler, a petty thug,
who bought a chain of chopsuey joints
in Piss River, Oregon,
with bootlegged Gucci cash.
Nobody dared question his integrity given

his nice, devout daughters
and his bright, industrious sons
as if filial piety were the standard
by which all earthly men were measured.

■

Oh, how trustworthy our daughters,
how thrifty our sons!
How we've managed to fool the experts
in education, statistics and demography—
We're not very creative but not adverse to rote-learning.
Indeed, they can *use* us.
But the "Model Minority" is a tease.
We know you are watching now,
so we refuse to give you any!
Oh, bamboo shoots, bamboo shoots!
The further west we go, we'll hit east;
The deeper down we dig, we'll find China.
History has turned its stomach
on a black polluted beach—
where life doesn't hinge
on that red, red wheelbarrow
but whether or not our new lover
in the final episode of "Santa Barbara"
will lean over a scented candle
and call us a "bitch."
Oh God, where have we gone wrong?
We have no inner resources!

■

Then, one redolent spring morning
the Great Patriarch Chin
peered down from his kiosk in heaven

and saw that his descendants were ugly.
One had a squarish head and a nose without a bridge.
Another's profile—long and knobbed as a gourd.
A third, the sad, brutish one
may never, never marry.
And I, his least favorite—
"not quite boiled, not quite cooked,"
a plump pomfret simmering in my juices—
too listless to fight for my people's destiny.
"To kill without resistance is not slaughter"
says the proverb. So, I wait for imminent death.
The fact that this death is also metaphorical
is testament to my lethargy.

So here lies Marilyn Mei Ling Chin,
married once, twice to so-and-so, a Lee and a Wong,
granddaughter of Jack "the patriarch"
and the brooding Suilin Fong,
daughter of the virtuous Yuet Kuen Wong
and G. G. Chin the infamous,
sister of a dozen, cousin of a million,
survived by everybody and forgotten by all.
She was neither black nor white,
neither cherished nor vanquished,
just another squatter in her own bamboo grove
minding her poetry—
when one day heaven was unmerciful,
and a chasm opened where she stood.
Like the jowls of a mighty white whale,
or the jaws of a metaphysical Godzilla,
it swallowed her whole.
She did not flinch nor writhe,
nor fret about the afterlife,

but stayed! Solid as wood, happily
a little gnawed, tattered, mesmerized
by all that was lavished upon her
and all that was taken away!

A BREAK IN THE RAIN
(or: Shall we meet again on Angel Island?)

Better Squat

Better squat than sit—
   sitting is too comfortable.
Better squat than stand—
   standing is too expectant.
Better squat and wait—
   as many have done before you,
head bent, knees hugged, body curled.

Better Play

And after all,
it is only Ping-Pong,
a game,
one to a side,
fixed points & boundaries,
a net that divides.
You needn't talent
or money,
only a green table
& white balls.
At first you play at the Y,
perhaps later
at Julie's or Mary's
in a freshly paneled room,
should you be invited.

Better Dance

With the one named Rochester
who likes your kind.

Let us dub him
"the point of entry."
Suddenly, he notices
your latticed hair.

Better Wait

The queues are long
& the amenities spare.

But *do* play.
Play,
dance, sing,
wait for a break in the rain.

TIANANMEN, THE AFTERMATH

There was blood and guts all over the road.
I said I'm sorry, darling, and rolled over,
expecting the slate to be clean; but she came,
she who was never alive became resurrected.
I saw her in dream . . . a young girl in a *qipao*,
Bespectacled, forever lingering, thriving
on the other side of the world, walking in my soles
as I walk, crying in my voice as I cried. When
she arrived, I felt my knuckles in her knock,
her light looming over the city's great hollows.

Hope lies within another country's semaphores.
The Goddess of Liberty, the Statue of Mercy—
we have it all wrong—big boy, how we choose to love,
how we choose to destroy, says Zhuangzi is written
in heaven—but leave the innocent ones alone,
those alive, yet stillborn, undead, yet waiting
in a fitful sleep undeserved of an awakening.

GRUEL

Your name is Diana Toy.
And all you may have for breakfast is rice gruel.
You can't spit it back into the cauldron for it would be unfilial.
You can't ask for yam gruel for there is none.
You can't hide it in the corner for it would surely be found
and then you would be served cold, stale rice gruel.

This is the philosophy of your tong:
you, the child, must learn to understand the universe
through the port-of-entry, your mouth,
to discern bitter from sweet, pungent from bland.
You were told that the infant Buddha once devoured earth
and spewed forth the wisdom of the ages.

Meat or gruel, wine or ghee,
even if it's gruel, even if it's nothing,
that gruel, that nothingness will shine
into the oil of your mother's scrap-iron wok,
into the glare of your father's cleaver,
and dance in your porcelain bowl.

Remember, what they deny you won't hurt you.
What they spare you, you must make shine,
so shine, shine . . .

BARBARIAN SUITE

for David Wong Louie

I.

The Ming will be over to make way for the Qing.
The Qing will be over to make way for eternity.
The East is red and the sun is rising.
All bleeds into the ocean in the Califia west.
My loss is your loss, a dialect here, a memory there—
if my left hand is dying will my right hand cut it off?
We shall all be vestigial organs, the gift of democracy.
The pale faces, the wan conformity,
the price we pay for comfort is our mother tongue.

II.

China is an ocean away, our grandmother beaconing
with too many children, too many mouths to feed.
We can no longer dress her and improve her accent.
We can no longer toil in her restaurant "Double Happiness,"
    oiling woks, peeling shrimp.
She is the bridge—and we've broken her back with our weight.
We study Western philosophy and explore our raison d'être.
All is well in the suburbs when we are in love with poetry.

III.

What did ya think, the emperor will come to your grave?
To tell ya all is groovy in the hinterlands?
What did ya think? Life's that hunky-dory?
What did ya expect, old peasant, old fool,
one day out of the woods and the dirt will eject
    from your nostrils?
Even dung-heaps will turn fragrant with a thorough cleansing?

IV.

Orchids doth not bloom, baby, they cry, they explode.
Meanwhile our anger gets muted in their fatal beauty—
AmerAsia so harmonious under a canopy of stars.
The pram of a new nation, the winds rock it gently.
Truth has no face, we make it wear ours.
You walk on the beach with your beautiful son Julian.
We dare to eat peaches and discuss the classics.

V.

One day they came to me, my dead ancestors.
They whispered *sse-sse-sse*, homophonous with "death."
I was under the covers with my barbarian boyfriend,
blowing smoke rings, talking jazz—"Posterity"
is yet another "compromising position,"
      addenda to the Kama Sutra.
I was playing Goddess/Dominatrix
and kept a piece of his ear as offering.

VI.

Cauldron full, cauldron empty.
The duck dangling in the window is the last vestige
      of our sizzling suzerainty.
They believed in order, which meant victory over oblivion.
They believed in the restaurant called "Double Happiness,"
where all the partners were brothers, all the sisters wore brocade.
The cash register rang its daily prayer wheels
      for the dying and the saved.

THE PHOENIX GONE, THE TERRACE EMPTY

川 流 不 息
The river flows without ceasing

Shallow river, shallow river,
these stairs are steep,
one foot, another,
I gather the hem
of my terry-cloth robe.
Quietly,
gingerly,
if an inch could sing
I would sing
for miles—
past the courtyard,
past the mulberries,
past the Bodhi tree
fragrant with jossticks,
past the Buddha
whose laughter is unmerciful.
Saunter,
my pink horses,
my tiny soldiers.
Heartbeat, hoofbeat,
softly,
gingerly,
do not disturb
the nasturtium,
do not ruin the irises
they planted.
In the rock garden
the flagstones
caress my feet,
kiss them tenderly.

"Who in the netherworld
walks on my soles
as I walk?
And opens her black mouth
when I cry?
Whose lutestrings
play my sorrow?
Whose silence
undulates
a millennium
of bells,
in which
all of history
shall wallow?

The banister
painted with red lacquer
where
my grip turns white.
These plum blossoms,
stock signifiers,
mocking my own ripeness
I cannot taste.
Flesh remembers
what the mind resists.
I think of
love
or the warm blur,
my mother—
I remember hate,
the hard shape,
my father.
They, slow moving,
mugworts,

no, water bison,
discuss my future
in a fulcrum
of angry gestures.
They shall come,
they shall come,
for our tithes.
She, my grandmother,
oiling her shuttle,
sings a lullaby
in an ancient falsetto,
In the east, a pink sash,
a girl has run away
from her mother.
He, my grandfather,
itinerant tinkerer,
heaves
his massive bellows.
His ember of hope flickering
in the village's
eternal sepulchre.
Do you remember
the shanty towns
on the hills of Wanchai,
tin roofs
crying into the sun?
Do you remember
Mother's first lover,
hurling
a kerosene lamp
into a hovel?
Ooooh, I can smell
the charred sweetness
in his raven hair.
The hills ablaze

with mayflies
and night-blooming jasmine.

Open the gate,
open,
the gilded facade
of restaurant "Double Happiness."
The man crouched
on the dirty linoleum
fingering dice
is my father.
He says:
"Mei Ling, child,
Mei Ling, don't cry,
I can change our lives
with one strike."

Do you know the stare
of a dead man?
My father the ox,
without his yoke,
sitting on a ridge
of the quay.
Auntie Jade
remembers:
"Hunger
had spooned
the flesh
from his cheeks.
His tuft
of black hair
was his only movement.
That Chinaman
Had no ideals,
no beliefs,

his dreams
were robbed
by the Japanese,
his fortune
was plundered
by the Nationalists,
the Communists
seared his home.
Misery had propped him there.
When you pray
to your ancestors
you are praying
to his hollowness."
Amaduofu, amaduofu—
child, child,
they cried.
"Ten thousand years of history and you have come to this.
Four thousand years of tutelage and you have come to this!"

Shall I walk
into the new world
in last year's pinafore?
Chanel says:
black, black
is our century's color.
Proper and elegant,
slim silhouette,
daywear and nightwear,
for parties and death,
and deep, deep regret.

"So, you've come home
finally
with your new boyfriend.
What is his name?

Ezekiel!
Odd name for a boy.
Your mother can't pronounce it.
And she doesn't like
his demeanor.
Too thin, too sallow,
he does not eat beef
in a country
where beef is possible.
He cannot play the violin
in a country
where rapture is possible.
He beams a tawdry smile,
perhaps he is hiding
bad intentions.
And that Moon
which accompanied his arrival,
that Moon won't drink
and is shaped naughtily
like a woman's severed ear."

The snake bites her own tail,
meaning harmony, at the year's end.
Or does it mean
she is eating herself
into extinction?

Oh dead prince, Oh hateful love,
shall we meet again
on the bridge of magpies?
Will you kiss me tenderly
where arch meets toe meets ankle,
where dried blood warbles?

Little bird, little bird,
Something escaping,
Something escaping . . .

The phoenix gone, the terrace empty.
Look, Mei Ling,
yellow crowfoot in the pond,
not lotus, not lily.

MOON AND OATGRASS

The moon is not over the water,
as you would have it,
but one with it, and the house
is on the precipice
overlooking a green meadow.
And you—and *eye* and not an *I*—
are walking through it.

And whether you live here
or are visiting
in your long pilgrimage—
is my prerogative.
Whether she is your acolyte,
the Pearl Concubine,
or a mere beggar woman—
is also my invention.

Only I know where
terrace ends and house begins,
whether the country is lost,
whether rivers and mountains
will continue. And finally,

after the inkstone is dry,
we shall be together
high in a corner bedroom
with a pale view of hills.
Without pleasure or transcendence
we penetrate this landscape.

And what *is* this landscape?
The moon in oatgrass,

the oatgrass moon.
A woman pacing
the linoleum floor,
contemplating a poem.
A man dissolving
into the dailyness of rain

and the red eye of morning.

HIS PARENTS' BAGGAGE

When we first met he had nothing,
naked as a brand-new lamb.
Fresh dew shimmered on the wool of his back.
Then, slowly, my small apartment filled
with meaningful gimcrack of his past.
And then, his parents' baggage . . .

First, his mother's small leathers:
prim, expensive, with a good name,
filled to the brim, ready to explode.
Took three friends to sit them closed.

Then his father's soft naugahyde:
one special piece, a suit-bag hung
over the doorjamb like a fresh carcass
picked open by private vultures.
And he and his sisters were the last
worms to clean the ribs.

I beg the question: who is host, who is guest?
Who the eater, who the eaten?
And in the depth of night,
in the wake of our dreams,
I reach out my arms to embrace what is left.

THE SURVIVOR

Don't tap your chopsticks against your bowl.
Don't throw your teacup against the wall in anger.
Don't suck on your long black braid and weep.
Don't tarry around the big red sign that says "danger!"

All the tempests will render still; seas will calm,
horses will retreat, voices to surrender.

That you have bloomed this way and not that,
that your skin is yellow, not white, not black,
that you were born not a boy-child but a girl,
that this world will be forever puce-pink are just as well.

Remember, the survivor is not the strongest nor most clever.
The survivor is almost always the youngest.
And you shall have to relinquish that title before long.

ALBA

White moon, white blossoms, white milky way,
White, white, morning of December.
Last night's candle has burned to a nub,
But she does not need another;
The snow outside her window is her guiding light.
Diana yearns to follow the old masters now,
Cuts four parallel lines into her heart.
You ask: why not a peony or a harmonious rainbow?
For the pattern of death should be exacting
As the rituals of life. So, do not mourn her.
You never shed a tear into her tin cup of living.
Tears would be spit now on the grave of the dead.

COMPOSED NEAR THE BAY BRIDGE

(after a wild party)

1)

Amerigo has his finger on the pulse of China.
He, Amerigo, is dressed profoundly punk:
Mohawk-pate, spiked dog collar, black leather thighs.
She, China, freshly hennaed and boaed, is intrigued
with the new diaspora and the sexual freedom
called *bondage*. "Isn't *bondage*, therefore,
a *kind* of freedom?" she asks, wanly.

2)

Thank God there was no war tonight.
Head-bent, Amerigo plucks his bad guitar.
The Sleeping Giant snores with her mouth agape
while a lone nightingale trills on a tree.

Through the picture window, I watch the traffic
hone down to a quiver. Loneliness. Dawn.
A few geese winging south; minor officials return home.

SUMMER LOVE

The black smoke rising means that I am cooking
dried lotus, bay oysters scrambled with eggs.
If this doesn't please you, too bad, it's all I have.
I don't mind your staying for breakfast—but, please—do not linger;
nothing worse in the morning than last night's love.

Your belly is flat and your skin—milk in the moonlight.
I notice your glimmer among a thousand tired eyes.
When we dance closely, fog thickens, all distinctions falter.
I let you touch me where I am most vulnerable,
heart of the vulva, vulva of the heart.

Perhaps, I fear, there will not be another like you.
Or you might walk away in the same face of the others—
    —blue with scorn and a troubled life.
But, for now, let the summers be savored and the centuries be forgiven—
two lovers in a field of floss and iris—
our freedom beaconing in dew and light.

TURTLE SOUP

You go home one evening tired from work,
and your mother boils you turtle soup.
Twelve hours hunched over the hearth
(who knows what else is in that cauldron).

You say, "Ma, you've poached the symbol of long life;
that turtle lived four thousand years, swam
the Wei, up the Yellow, over the Yangtze.
Witnessed the Bronze Age, the High Tang,
grazed on splendid sericulture."
(So, she boils the life out of him.)

"All our ancestors have been fools.
Remember Uncle Wu who rode ten thousand miles
to kill a famous Manchu and ended up
with his head on a pole? Eat, child,
its liver will make you strong."

"Sometimes you're the life, sometimes the sacrifice."
Her sobbing is inconsolable.
So, you spread the gentle napkin
over your lap in decorous Pasadena.

Baby, some high priestess got it wrong.
The golden decal on the green underbelly
says "Made in Hong Kong."

Is there nothing left but the shell
and humanity's strange inscriptions,
the songs, the rites, the oracles?

A PORTRAIT OF THE SELF AS NATION, 1990–1991

Fit in dominata servitus
In servitude dominatus
In mastery there is bondage
In bondage there is mastery
            (Latin proverb)

The stranger and the enemy
We have seen him in the mirror.
            (George Seferis)

Forgive me, Head Master,
but you see, I have forgotten
to put on my black lace underwear, and instead
I have hiked my slip up, up to my waist
so that I can enjoy the breeze.
It feels good to be *without*,
so good as to be salacious.
The feeling of flesh kissing tweed.
If ecstasy had a color, it would be
yellow and pink, yellow and pink
Mongolian skin rubbed raw.
The serrated lining especially fine
like wearing a hair-shirt, inches above the knee.
When was the last time I made love?
The last century? With a wan missionary.
Or was it San Wu the Bailiff?
The tax collector who came for my tithes?
The herdboy, the ox, on the bridge of magpies?
It was Roberto, certainly,
high on coke, circling the galaxy.
Or my recent vagabond love
driving a reckless chariot, lost
in my feral country. *Country*, Oh I am

so punny, so very, very punny.
Dear Mr. Decorum, don't you agree?

It's not so much the length of the song
but the range of the emotions—Fear
has kept me a good pink monk—and poetry
is my nunnery. Here I am alone in my altar,
self-hate, self-love, both self-erotic notions.
Eyes closed, listening to that one hand clapping—
not metaphysical trance, but fleshly mutilation—
and loving *it*, myself and that pink womb, my bed.
Reading "Jing Ping Mei" in the "expurgated"
where all the female protagonists were named
Lotus.
Those damned licentious women named us
Modest, Virtue, Cautious, Endearing,
Demure-dewdrop, Plum-aster, Petal-stamen.
They teach us to walk head-bent in devotion,
to honor the five relations, ten sacraments.
Meanwhile, the feast is brewing elsewhere,
the ox is slaughtered and her entrails are hung
on the branches for the poor. They convince us, yes,
our chastity will save the nation—Oh mothers,
all your sweet epithets didn't make us wise!
Orchid by any other name is equally seditious.

Now, where was I, oh yes, now I remember,
the last time I made love, it was to *you.*
I faintly remember your whiskers
against my tender nape.
You were a conquering barbarian,
helmeted, halberded,
beneath the gauntleted moon,
whispering Hunnish or English—
so-long Oolong went the racist song,

bye-bye little chinky butterfly.
There is no cure for self-pity,
the disease is death,
ennui, disaffection,
a roll of flesh-colored tract homes crowding my imagination.
I do hate my loneliness,
sitting cross-legged in my room,
satisfied with a few off-rhymes,
sending off precious haiku to some inconspicuous journal
named "Left Leaning Bamboo."
You, my precious reader, O sweet voyeur,
sweaty, balding, bespectacled,
in a rumpled rayon shirt
and a neo-Troubadour chignon,
politics mildly centrist,
the *right* fork for the *right* occasions,
matriculant of the best schools—
herewith, my last confession
(with decorous and perfect diction)
I loathe to admit. Yet, I shall admit it:
there was no Colonialist coercion;
sadly, we blended together well.
I was poor, starving, war torn,
an empty coffin to be filled.
You were a young, ambitious Lieutenant
with dreams of becoming Prince
of a "new world order," Lord
over the League of Nations.

Lover, destroyer, savior!
I remember that moment of beguilement,
one hand muffling my mouth,
one hand untying my sash—
On your throat dangled a golden cross.
Your god is jealous, your god is cruel.

So, when did you finally return?
And . . . was there a second coming?
My memory is failing me, perhaps
you came too late
(we were already dead).
Perhaps you didn't come at all—
you had a deadline to meet,
another alliance to secure,
another resistance to break.
Or you came too often
to my painful dismay.
(Oh, how facile the liberator's hand.)
Often when I was asleep
You would hover over me
with your great silent wingspan
and watch me sadly.
This is the way you want me—
asleep, quiescent, almost dead,
sedated by lush immigrant dreams
of global bliss, connubial harmony.

Yes, I shall always remember
and deign to forgive
(long before I am satiated,
long before I am spent)
that last pressured cry,
"your little death."
Under the halcyon light
you would smoke and contemplate
the sea and debris,
that barbaric keening
of what it means to be free.
As if we were ever free,
as if ever we could be.
Said the judge,

"Congratulations,
On this day, fifteen of November, 1967,
Marilyn Mei Ling Chin,
application # z-z-z-z-z,
you are an American citizen,
naturalized in the name of God
the father, God the son and the Holy Ghost."
Time assuages, and even
the Yellow River becomes clean . . .

Meanwhile we forget
the power of exclusion,
what you are walling in or out—
and to whom you must give offense.
The hungry, the slovenly, the convicts
need not apply.
The syphilitic, the consumptive
may not moor.
The hookwormed and tracomaed
(and the likewise infested).
The gypsies, the sodomists, the mentally infirm.
The pagans, the heathens, the non-
denominational—
The colored, the mixed-races and the reds.
The communists, the usurious,
the mutants, the Hibakushas, the hags . . .

Oh, connoisseurs of gastronomy and *keemun* tea!
My foes, my loves,
how eloquent your discrimination,
how precise your poetry.
Last night, in our large, rotund bed,
we witnessed the fall. *Ours*
was an "aerial war." Bombs
glittering in the twilight sky

against the Star-Spangled Banner.
Dunes and dunes of sand,
fields and fields of rice.
A thousand charred oil wells,
the firebrands of night.
Ecstasy made us tired.

Sir, Master, Dominatrix,
Fall was a glorious season for the hegemonists.
We took long melancholy strolls on the beach,
digressed on art and politics
in a quaint wharfside café in La Jolla.
The storm grazed our bare arms gently . . .
History has never failed us.
Why save Babylonia or Cathay,
when we can always have Paris?
Darling, if we are to remember it at all,
Let us remember it well—
We were fierce, yet tender,
fierce and tender.

SONG OF THE SAD GUITAR

In the bitter year of 1988 I was banished to San Diego, California, to become a wife there. It was summer. I was buying groceries under the Yin and Yang sign of Safeway. In the parking lot, the puppies were howling to a familiar tune on a guitar plucked with the zest and angst of the sixties. I asked the player her name.

She answered:
"Stone Orchid, but if you call me that, I'll kill you."
I said:
"Yes, perhaps stone is too harsh for one with a voice so pure."
She said:
"It's the 'orchid' I detest; it's prissy, cliché and forever pink."

From my shopping bag I handed her a Tsingtao and urged her to play on.

She sang about hitchhiking around the country, moons and lakes, homeward-honking geese, scholars who failed their examination. Men leaving for war; women climbing the watchtower. There were courts, more courts and inner-most courts, and scions who pillaged the country.

Suddenly, I began to feel deeply about my own banishment. The singer I could have been, what the world looked like in spring, that Motown collection I lost. I urged her to play on:

> *Trickle, Trickle, the falling rain.*
> *Ming, ming, a deer lost in the forest.*
> *Surru, surru, a secret conversation.*
> *Hung, hung, a dog in the yard.*

Then, she changed her mood, to a slower lament, trilled a song macabre, about death, about a guitar case that opened like a coffin. Each string vibrant, each note a thought. Tell me, Orchid, where are we going? "The book of changes does not signify change. The laws are immutable. Our fates are sealed." Said Orchid—the song is a dirge and an awakening.

Two years after our meeting, I became deranged. I couldn't cook, couldn't clean. My house turned into a pigsty. My children became delinquents. My husband began a long lusty affair with another woman. The house burned during a feverish *Santa Ana* as I sat in a pink cranny above the garage singing, "At twenty, I marry you. At thirty, I begin hating everything that you do."

One day while I was driving down Mulberry Lane, a voice came over the radio. It was Stone Orchid. She said, "This is a song for an old friend of mine. Her name is Mei Ling. She's a warm and sensitive housewife now living in Hell's Creek, California. I've dedicated this special song for her, 'The Song of the Sad Guitar.'"

I am now beginning to understand the song within the song, the weeping within the willow. And you, out there, walking, talking, seemingly alive—may truly be dead and waiting to be summoned by the sound of the sad guitar.

for Maxine Hong Kingston

BEIJING SPRING

Love, if I could give you the eternal summer sun
or China back her early ideological splendor, I would.
If I could hoist the dead horses back
and retrieve the wisdom charred by the pyres of Qin.
If I could give mother the Hong Kong of her mulberry youth
and father the answer that the ox desired,
they would still be together now and not blame
their sadness on the unyielding earth.
If I had separated goose from gander, goose from gander,
the question of breeding for life, the question
of the pure yellow seed would not enter.

This courtyard, this fortress,
this alluvium where the dead leave their faces—
each step I take erases the remnants of another,
each song I sing obfuscates the song of Changan,
ripples washing sand, ripples washing sand, ripples . . .
each poem I write conjures the dead washing women of Loyang.

Lover, on Tiananmen Square, near the Avenue of Eternal Peace,
I believe in the passions of youth,
I believe in eternal spring.
As the white blossoms, sweet harbingers,
pull a wreath around the city,
as heaven spreads its indifference over
the bloodied quay, I want to hold you
against the soft silhouettes of my people.
Let me place my mouth over your mouth,
let me breathe life into your life,
let me summon the paired connubial geese
from the far reaches of the galaxy
to soar over the red spokes of the sun's slow chariot
and begin again.

AUTUMN LEAVES

The dead piled up, thick, fragrant, on the fire escape.
My mother ordered me again, and again, to sweep it clean.
All that blooms must fall. I learned this not from the Dao,
　　but from high school biology.

Oh, the contradictions of having a broom and not a dustpan!
I swept the leaves down, down through the iron grille
and let the dead rain over the Wong family's patio.

And it was Achilles Wong who completed the task.
　　We called her:
The one-who-cleared-away-another-family's-autumn.
She blossomed, tall, benevolent, notwithstanding.

THE FLORAL APRON

The woman wore a floral apron around her neck,
that woman from my mother's village
with a sharp cleaver in her hand.
She said, "What shall we cook tonight?
Perhaps these six tiny squid
lined up so perfectly on the block?"

She wiped her hand on the apron,
pierced the blade into the first.
There was no resistance,
no blood, only cartilage
soft as a child's nose. A last
iota of ink made us wince.

Suddenly, the aroma of ginger and scallion fogged our senses,
and we absolved her for that moment's barbarism.
Then, she, an elder of the tribe,
without formal headdress, without elegance,
deigned to teach the younger
about the Asian plight.

And although we have traveled far
we must never forget that primal lesson
—on patience, courage, forbearance,
on how to love squid despite squid,
how to honor the village, the tribe,
that floral apron.

FROM

RHAPSODY IN PLAIN YELLOW (2002)

THAT HALF IS ALMOST GONE

That half is almost gone,
                    the Chinese half,
the fair side of a peach,
                    darkened by the knife of time,
fades like a cruel sun.

In my thirtieth year
                    I wrote a letter to my mother.

I had forgotten the character
                    for "love." I remember vaguely
the radical "heart."
                    The ancestors won't fail to remind you

the vital and vestigial organs
                    where the emotions come from.

        But the rest is fading.
                    A slash dissects in midair,
ai, ai, ai, ai,
                    more of a cry than a sigh

(and no help from the phoneticist).

        You are a Chinese!
                    My mother was adamant.

        You *are* a Chinese?
                    My mother less convinced.

        Are you *not* Chinese?
                    My mother now accepting.

As a cataract clouds her vision,
                                and her third daughter marries
a Protestant West Virginian

                    who is "very handsome and very kind."

The mystery is still unsolved—

                                the landscape looms

over man. And the gaffer-hatted fishmonger—

                                        sings to his cormorant.

And the maiden behind the curtain

                            is somebody's courtesan.

Or, merely Rose Wong's aging daughter

                        Pondering the blue void.

You are a Chinese—said my mother
                        who once walked the fields of her dead—

Today, on the 36th anniversary of my birth,

I have problems now
                    even with the salutation.

THE COLONIAL LANGUAGE IS ENGLISH

Heaven manifests its duality
My consciousness on earth is twofold
My parents speak with two tongues
My mother's tongue is Toisan
My father's tongue is Cantonese
The colonial language is English
I and thou, she and thee
My mother is of two minds
The village and the family
My mother loves me, I am certain
She molded my happiness in her womb
My mother loves my brother, certainly
His death was not an enigma
Yet, it, too, had its mystery

I had willed it in my heart
I had condemned him in his crib
When I touched his round, Buddha face
Drank in his soft, infant beauty
Cain and Abel had a sister
Her name is Tiny Pearl
Too precious to be included in their story
Her small throat trilled in vain
The Dao of which we speak is not the eternal Dao
The name that we utter is not the eternal name
My mother is me, my father is thee
As we drown in the seepage of Sutter Mill

BLUES ON YELLOW

The canary died in the gold mine, her dreams got lost in the sieve.
The canary died in the gold mine, her dreams got lost in the sieve.
Her husband the crow killed under the railroad, the spokes hath shorn his
*   wings.*

Something's cookin' in Chin's kitchen, ten thousand yellow-bellied sapsuckers
*   baked in a pie.*
Something's cookin' in Chin's kitchen, ten thousand yellow-bellied sapsuckers
*   baked in a pie.*
Something's cookin' in Chin's kitchen, die die yellow bird, die die.

O crack an egg on the griddle, yellow will ooze into white.
O crack an egg on the griddle, yellow will ooze into white.
Run, run, sweet little Puritan, yellow will ooze into white.

If you cut my yellow wrists, I'll teach my yellow toes to write.
If you cut my yellow wrists, I'll teach my yellow toes to write.
If you cut my yellow fists, I'll teach my yellow feet to fight.

Do not be afraid to perish, my mother, Buddha's compassion is nigh.
Do not be afraid to perish, my mother, our boat will sail tonight.
Your babies will reach the promised land, the stars will be their guide.

I am so mellow yellow, mellow yellow, Buddha sings in my veins.
I am so mellow yellow, mellow yellow, Buddha sings in my veins.
O take me to the land of the unreborn, there's no life on earth without pain.

CHINESE QUATRAINS (THE WOMAN IN TOMB 44)

The aeroplane is shaped like a bird
Or a giant mechanical penis
My father escorts my mother
From girlhood to unhappiness

A dragonfly has iridescent wings
Shorn, it's a lowly pismire
Plucked of arms and legs
A throbbing red pepperpod

Baby, she's a girl
Pinkly propped as a doll
Baby, she's a pearl
An ulcer in the oyster of God

Cry little baby clam cry
The steam has opened your eyes
Your secret darkly hidden
The razor is sharpening the knife

Abandoned taro-leaf boat
Its lonely black sail broken
The corpses are fat and bejeweled
The hull is thoroughly rotten

The worm has entered the ear
And out the nose of my father
Cleaned the pelvis of my mother
And ringed around her fingerbone

One child beats a bedpan
One beats a fishhook out of wire
One beats his half sister on the head
Oh, teach us to fish and love

Don't say her boudoir is too narrow
She could sleep but in one cold bed
Don't say you own many horses
We escaped on her skinny mare's back

Man is good said Mengzi
We must cultivate their natures
Man is evil said Xunzi
There's a worm in the human heart

He gleaned a beaded purse from Hong Kong
He procured an oval fan from Taiwan
She married him for a green card
He abandoned her for a blonde

My grandmother is calling her goslings
My mother is summoning her hens
The sun has vanished into the ocean
The moon has drowned in the fen

Discs of jade for her eyelids
A lozenge of pearl for her throat
Lapis and kudzu in her nostrils
They will rob her again and again

TAKE A LEFT AT THE WATERS OF SAMSARA

There is a bog of sacred water
      Behind a hedgerow of wild madder
Near the grave of my good mother
      Tin cans blossom there

The rust shimmers like amber
      A diorama of green gnats
Ecstatic in their veil dance
      A nation of frogs regale

Swell-throated, bass-toned
      One belts and rages, the others follow
They fuck blissfully
      Trapped in their cycle

Of rebirth, transient love
      Unprepared for higher ground
And I, my mother's aging girl
      Myopic, goat-footed

Got snagged on an unmarked trail
      The road diverged; I took
The one less traveled
      Blah, blah

I sit at her grave for hours
      A slow drizzle purifies my flesh
I still yearn for her womb
      And can't detach

I chant new poems, my best fascicle
        Stupid pupil, the truth
Is an oxymoron and exact
        Eternity can't be proven to the dead

What is the void but motherlessness?
        The song bellies up
The sun taketh
        The rain ceases to bless

MILLENNIUM, SIX SONGS

I.

Black swollen fruit dangling on a limb
Red forgotten flesh sprayed across the prairie
Parched brown vines creeping over the wall
Yellow winged pollen, invisible enemies

Boluses without homesteads, grubs without a voice
Burrowed deeply into this land's dark, dark heart
Someday, our pods and pupae shall turn in the earth
And burgeon into our motherlode's bold beauty

II.

We're a seed on the manure, on the sole of your shoe
We're the louse trapped in your hank of golden hair
We're the sliver that haunts beneath your thumbnail
We're the church mouse you scorched with a match but lived

We're the package wrapped, return address unknown
We're the arm lowered again, again, a bloodied reverie
We've arrived shoeless, crutchless, tousle-haired, swollen-bellied
We shall inherit this earth's meek glory, as foretold

III. (FOR MY NIECE, LEAH)

They gave you a title, but you were too proud to wear it
They gave you the *paterland*, but you were too lazy to farm it

Your condo is leaking, but you're too angry to repair it
Your dress has moth holes, but you're too sentimental to toss it

You're too bored to play the lute, it hangs on the wall like an ornament
The piano bites you, it's an eight-legged unfaithful dog

Love grows in the garden, but you're too impudent to tend it
A nice Hakka boy from Ogden, so hardworking, so kind

The prayer mat is for prayer, not for catamite nipple-piercing
The Goddess wags her finger at your beautiful wasteland

A dream deferred, well, is a dream deferred

IV. (JANIE'S RETORT, ON HER FORTIETH BIRTHDAY)

The same stars come around and around and around
The same sun peeks her head at the horizon
The same housing tract, the same shopping center
The same blunt haircut: Chinese Parisian, Babylonian
The same lipstick: red and it comes off on your coffee cup
The same stars come around and around and around
The same sun tarries in the late noon sky
The same word for mom: *Ah ma, madre, mere, majka*
The same birth-babe: bald, purplish, you slap to make cry
The same stench: mother's milk, shit and vomit
The same argument between a man and a woman
The same dog, hit by a car, the same escaped canary
The same turkey for Thanksgiving, Christmas and the New Year
The same three-tiered freeway, Istanbul, Tokyo, San Diego
The same hill, the same shanty town, the same lean-to
The same skyscraper: Hong Kong, Singapore, Toledo
The same rice for supper: white, brown or wild
The same stars come around and around and around
The same sun dips her head into the ocean
The same tree in the same poem by the same poet
The same old husband: saggy breasts, baggy thighs
The same blackness whether we sleep or die

V.

Whoever abandoned her grandmother at the bus stop
Whoever ran in and out the door like a blind wind
    Spinning the upside-down prosperity sign   right side up again
Whoever lost her virtue   in darkly paneled rooms   with white boys
Whoever prayed for round eyes
    and taped her eyelids in waiting
Whoever wore platform shoes
    Blustering taller than her own kind
Whoever sold her yellow gold for Jehovah
Whoever discarded her jade Buddha for Christ

VI.

Why are you proud, father, entombed with the other woman?
Why are you proud, mother, knitting my shroud in heaven?
Why are you proud, fish, you feed the greedy mourners?
Why are you proud, millennium, the dialect will die with you?
Why are you proud, psalm, hammering yourself into light?

CAULDRON

General Yuan Shih Kai
your horse went mad.
He danced a ribbon
around the character for "chaos."
And oh, such a character
it was.
Oh grand master,
won't you let the light in.
This human destiny,
scroll and colophon,
painterly and evocative—
is the greatest masterpiece,
dark as it is.
There are horses and chariots,
Chin's terracotta soldiers,
vengeful pale ghosts.
The men—chivalrous and virile
behind forged armors.
The women—forebearers of sorrow
in soft cloud chignons.
The cauldron is heavy—
our bones will flavor the pottage,
our wrists will bear its signature.
As the kingdom's saga trills on,
familial and personal,
the great panorama of Loyang
blusters in its silent gallows
and the war-torn vermilion glow
of eternal summer.
There is my granduncle
plotting to sell my mother
for a finger of opium.

There is my grandmother
running after him, tottering
down the grassy knolls
in her bound feet
and unraveled hair.
Her cry would startle the ages.
Meanwhile, the chrysanthemum blooms
shamelessly, beautifully,
confident of a fast resolve.
Yes, all would fructify notwithstanding—
all that is beautiful must bloom,
all that blooms is beautiful.
My grandmother's cry would chill the gorges,
remembered by the caretaker of pines
in the Shaolin monastery
and the young boy taking the tonsure,
remembered by the blind sage Vitapithaca,
his acolyte the Monkey King,
the Sandman and the pusillanimous pig,
remembered by the Emperor of Heaven
and the Yellow Prince of Hell.
O Goddess of Mercy, why have you been remiss?
I have burnt joss sticks at your ivory feet.
I have kept the sanctity of my body
and the cleanliness of my mind.
I have washed my heart of bad intentions
And she hobbles, down past the oatgrass
Past the buffalo trough, past her lover,
whom she would not name,
past the priest and his valley of carillon,
and the red, red sorghum of her childhood.
Past the oxen and her family ox
in a rare moment without his yoke,
past the girls chattering behind the sassafras,
and the women bathing and threshing hemp.

Past the gaffer-hatted fisherman
and his song of the cormorant.
Oh shoulder thy burdens, old cudgel, shoulder them
in your brief moments of reprieve and splendor.
My grandmother ran, driven by the wind.
The pain in her hooves, those tender hooves
those painful lotuses could not deter her.
As the warlord's bamboo whip flailed
over the unyielding sky,
and the Japanese bayonets flash
against the ancient banyans,
all history would step aside, grant her passage.

What is destiny, but an angry wind—plagues and salvages,
death knocking on your neighbor's door, and you dare look out
your window, relieved that you were spared for another hour.

Gather your thoughts, brief butterfly, your water clock dries.
Shallow river, shallow river, how shall I cross?

Footsteps so light, the fallow deer can't hear her.
Heart so heavy, the village women would sink a stone
in her name each time they crossed the shoals.
The soothsayer in the watchtower espies her.
Oh destiny-in-a-whirlwind, serpent-in-the-grass,
she inches toward her ailing half-brother.
Dragging feudalism's gangrene legs,
their kind is wan and dying.
The child on his back, limp with exhaustion,
answers to my grandmother's call.

Night will lower its black knife,
only the lantern will bear witness now.
The bridge is crossed.   My mother is saved.
Her hemp doll dragged downstream by the river.

VARIATIONS ON AN ANCIENT THEME:
THE DRUNKEN HUSBAND

The dog is barking at the door
"Daddy crashed the car"
"Hush, kids, go to your room
Don't come out until it's over"
He stumbles up the dim-lit stairs
Drops his Levis to his ankles
"Touch me and I'll kill you," she says
Pointing a revolver at his head

The dog is barking at the door
She doesn't recognize the master
She sniffs his guilty crotch
Positioned to bite it off
"Jesus, control your dog
A man can't come back to his castle"
"Kill him, Ling Ling," she sobs
Curlers bobbing on her shoulders

The dog is barking at the door
"Quiet, Spot, let's not wake her"
The bourbon is sour on his breath
Lipstick on his proverbial collar
He turns on the computer in the den
He calms the dog with a bone
Upstairs, she sleeps, facing the wall
Dreaming about the Perfume River

The dog is barking at the door
He stumbles in swinging
"Where is my gook-of-a-wife
Where are my half-breed monsters?"
All is silent, up the cold stairs
No movement, no answer
The drawers are open like graves
The closets agape to the rafters

The dog is barking at the door
He stumbles in singing
"How is my teenage bride?
How is my mail-order darling?
Perhaps she's pretending to be asleep
Waiting for her man's hard cock"
He enters her from behind
Her sobbing does not deter him

The dog is barking at the door
What does the proud beast know?
Who is both Master and intruder?
Whose bloody handprint on the wall?
Whose revolver in the dishwater?
The neighbors won't heed her alarm
She keeps barking, barking
Bent on saving their kind

BOLD BEAUTY

She opened her eyes and he was already within her,
though the lore said that a mere kiss would suffice.
The song distorted on the tongue of the soothsayer—
no need to struggle, he would take her away
on his white, white steed and panniers of riches.
In veils and swathing she would be reborn as queen.

Out in the ramparts the last village seared.
Her parents cried out for their lost girlchild,
"Cai Yen, Cai Yen," but the sky did not answer.
Her thin jade bracelet shattered into five dazzling pieces,
one for each element that made up the stars.
A constellation of black hair was her last missive.

In antechamber and darkness she feels him again.
The tale is the rapture of the water clock, pain
which burns into pleasure, burns into the hours.
Our heroine turns over and slits the throat of her beloved.
She would avenge her family, her sovereignty, her dead.
She who survives to tell the tale shall hold the power.

THE TRUE STORY OF MORTAR AND PESTLE

for my sister, Jane

Nobody understood her cruelty to herself. In this life, cruelty begets cruelty, and before long, one would have to chop off one's own hand to end the source of self-torture. Yet, we continue, Sister Mortar pounding on Sister Pestle. The hand refuses to retreat, as if to retreat would mean less meat on the table.

She, Mortar, the presentable one: clean, well-kept, jade cross, white colonial pinafore, shiny knees and elbows, straight As, responsible hall monitor, future councilwoman. She is Yang: heaven, sunlight, vigorous, masculine, penetrator, the monad.

She, Pestle: disheveled, morose, soft-spoken, a fearful dark crucible. She is Yin: heaven's antithesis, moony, fecund, feminine, absorption, the duad.

The outer child had everything to live for: tenure, partnership in the firm, shapely breasts, strong legs, praise from a few key critics, the love of a good man.

The inner child was denied food, yet food was ample. She was denied sleep, yet darkness descended as day.

Justice was the hateful stepfather. His voice was loud, truculent in their ear, *If you succeed there would be no applause; if you fail, there, too, would be silent reckoning.*

Listen to that serious pounding of the ages . . . not nocturnal lovemaking of the muses, but the bad sister pounding the good. Somewhere in the scintillating powder we grind into light.

THE TRUE STORY OF MR. AND MRS. WONG

Mrs. Wong bore Mr. Wong four children, all girls.
One after the other, they dropped out like purple plums.
One night after long hours at the restaurant and a bad gambling bout
Mr. Wong came home drunk. He kicked the bedstead and shouted,
"What do you get from a turtle's rotten womb but rotten turtle eggs?"
So, in the next two years he quickly married three girls off to a missionary,
a shell-shocked ex-Marine and an anthropologist. The youngest ran away
to Hollywood and became a successful sound specialist.

Mr. Wong said to Mrs. Wong, "Look what happened to my progeny.
My ancestors in heaven are ashamed. I am a rich man now. All the
Chinese restaurants in San Jose are named Wong. Yet, you couldn't offer
me a healthy son. I must change my fate, buy myself a new woman. She
must have fresh eggs, white and strong." So, Mr. Wong divorced Mrs.
Wong, gave her a meager settlement and sent her back to Hong Kong,
where she lived to a ripe old age as the city's corpse beautician.

Two years ago, Mr. Wong became a born-again Christian. He now loves
his new wife, whose name is Mrs. Fuller-Wong. At first she couldn't
conceive. Then, the Good Lord performed a miracle and removed three
large polyps from her womb. She bore Mr. Wong three healthy sons
and they all became corporate tax accountants.

TONIGHT WHILE THE STARS ARE SHIMMERING
(New World Duet)

A burst of red hibiscus on the hill
                     A dahlia-blue silence chills the path
Compassion falters on Highway 8
                     Between La Jolla and Julian you are sad
Across the Del Mar shores I ponder my dead mother
                     Between heaven and earth, a pesky brown gull
The sky is green where it meets the ocean
                     You're the master of subterfuge, my love
A plume of foul orange from a duster plane
                     I wonder what poison he is releasing, you say
A steep wall of wildflowers, perhaps verbena
                     Purple so bright they mock the robes of God

In Feudal China you would've been drowned at birth
                     In India charred for a better dowry
How was I saved on that boat of freedom
                     To be anointed here on the prayer mat of your love?
High humidity, humiliation on the terrain
                     Oi, you can't describe the ocean to the well frog
I call you racist, you call me racist
                     Now, we're entering forbidden territory
I call you sexist, you call me a fool
                     And compare the canyons to breasts, anyway
I pull your hair, you bite my nape
                     We make mad love until birdsong morning

You tear off your shirt, you cry out to the moon
                     In the avocado grove you find peaches
You curse on the precipice, I weep near the sea
                     The *Tribune* says NOBODY WILL MARRY YOU
YOU'RE ALREADY FORTY

My mother followed a cockcrow, my granny a dog
Their palms arranged my destiny
Look, there's Orion, look, the Dog Star
Sorry, your majesty, your poetry has lost its *duende*
Look, baby, baby, stop the car
A mouse and a kitty hawk, they are dancing

Yellow-mauve marguerites close their faces at dusk
Behind the iron gate, a jasmine breeze
In life we share a pink quilt, in death a blue vault
Shall we cease this redress, this wasteful ransom?
Your coffee is bitter, your spaghetti is sad
Is there no ending this colloquy?
Ms. Lookeast, Ms. Lookeast
What have we accomplished this century?

I take your olive branch deep within me
A white man's guilt, a white man's love
Tonight while the stars are shimmering

SO, YOU FUCKED JOHN DONNE

So, you fucked John Donne.
Wasn't very nice of you.
He was betrothed to God, you know,
a diet of worms for you!

So, you fucked John Keats.
He's got the sickness, you know.
You *took precautions*, you say.
So, you fucked him anyway.

John Donne, John Keats,
John Guevara, John Wong,
John Kennedy, Johnny John-John.
The beautiful, the reckless, the strong.

Poor thang, you had no self-worth then,
you fucked them all for a song.

GET RID OF THE X

My shadow followed me to San Diego
    silently, she never complained.
No green card, no identity pass,
    she is wedded to my fate.

The moon is drunk and anorexic,
    constantly reeling, changing weight.
My shadow dances grotesquely,
    resentful she can't leave me.

The moon mourns his unwritten novels,
    cries naked into the trees and fades.
Tomorrow, he'll return to beat me
    blue—again, again and again.

Goodbye Moon, goodbye Shadow.
    My husband, my lover, I'm late.
The sun will plunge through the window.
    I must make my leap of faith.

IDENTITY POEM (#99)

Are you the sky—or the allegory for loneliness?
Are you the only Chinese restaurant in Roseburg, Oregon?
A half-breed war orphan—adopted by proper Christians?

A heathen poidog, a creamy half-and-half?
Are you a dingy vinyl address book? A wrist
Without a corsage? Are you baby's breath

Faced down on a teenage road in America?
Are you earphones—detached
Left dangling on an airplane jack to diaspora?

Are you doomed to a childhood without music?
Weary of your granny's one-string, woe-be-gone *erhu*
Mewling about the past

Are you hate speech or are you a lullaby?
Anecdotes requiring footnotes
An ethnic joke rehashed

How many Chinamen does it take—to screw
How many Chinamen does it take—to screw
A lightbulb?

Are you so poor that you cannot call your mother?
You have less than two dollars on your phone-card
And it's a long cable to Nirvana

Are you a skylight through which the busgirl sees heaven?
A chopping block stained by the blood of ten thousand innocents
Which daily, the same busgirl must wipe off

Does existence preempt essence?
I "being" what my ancestors were not
Suddenly, you're a vegan vegetarian!

Restaurant is a facticity and
Getting the hell out—is transcendence
Was the punch line "incandescent"?

Was a nosebleed your last tender memory of her?
Did he say no dogs and Chinawomen?
Are you a rose—or a tattoo of fire?

TO PURSUE THE LIMITLESS

To pursue the limitless
With a hare-brained paramour
To chase a dull husband
With a sharp knife

To speak to Rose
About her thorny sisters
Lock the door behind you
The restaurant is on fire

You are named after
Flower and precious metal
You are touched
By mercury

Your birth-name is Dawning
Your milk-name is Twilight
Your betrothed name is Dusk

To speak in dainty aphorisms
To dither
In monosyllables
Binomes copulating in midair

To teach English as a second
Third, fourth language

You were faithful to the original
You were married to the Chinese paradox

美言不信　　信言不美

Beautiful words are not truthful
The truth is not beautiful

You have translated "bitter" as "melon"
"Fruit" as "willful absence"

You were mum as an egg
He was brutal as an embryo
Blood-soup will congeal in the refrigerator

You are both naturalized citizens
You have the right to a little ecstasy

To (二) err is human   To (五) woo is woman

Mái mā   埋媽   *buried Mother*
Mài má   賣麻   *sold hemp*
Mǎi mǎ   買馬   *bought horse*

No, not the tones but the tomes

You said *My name is Zhuàng Měi*   (壯美)
     Sturdy Beauty

But he thought you said *Shuāng Méi*   (霜梅)
     Frosty Plum

He brandished his arc of black hair like a coxcomb
He said *Meet me at the airport travelator*
His back door was lovelier than his front door

A smear of bile on your dress
Proved his existence

HORSE HORSE HYPHEN HYPHEN
Border Ghazals

I.

I hate, I love, I don't know how
I'm biracial, I'm torn in two

Tonight, he will lock me in fear
In the metal detector of love

Rapeflowers, rapeseeds, rapiers
A soldier's wry offerings

He will press his tongue
Into my neighing throat

I can speak three dialects badly
I want you now behind the blue door

In a slow hovercraft of dreams
I saw Nanking from a bilge

Some ashes fell on his lap
I'm afraid it's my mother

The protocol is never to mention her
While we are fucking

II.

The bad conceit, the bad conceit police will arrest you
Twin compasses, twin compasses cannot come

Your father is not a car, not a compass and not God
Though he vanished in his sky-blue convertible Galaxy with a blonde

He kept crawling back to us, back to us
Each time with a fresh foot mangled

One emperor was named Lickety, the other named Split
Suddenly, the soup of chaos makes sense

Refugees roaming from tent to tent to tent, looking for love
The banknote is a half note, an octave above God

O the great conjugator of curses: shit, shat, have shut!
I have loved you both bowl-cut and shagged

There are days when the sun is a great gash
Nights, the moon smokes hashish and falls asleep on your lap

Sorry, but your morphing was not satisfactory
Shapeshifter, you choked on your magic scarf

III.

I heard this joke at a bar
An agnostic dyslexic insomniac stayed up all night searching for doG

The prosperity sign flips right side up again
The Almanac says this Ox Year we'll toil like good immigrants

Horse is frigid. Mule can't love
Salmon dead at the redd

One leg is stationary, the other must tread, must tread, must tread
The Triads riddled him, then us

What is the heart's past participle?
She would have loved not to have loved

I bought you at the corner of *Agave* and *Revolucíon*
You wrapped yourself thrice around my green arm and shat!

A childless woman can feel the end of all existence
Look, on that bloody spot, Chrysanthemum!

Shamanka, fetch your grandmother at the bus stop
Changeling, you are the one I love

HOSPITAL INTERLUDE

I rented a red Miata   I returned to the hospital
I returned to the hospital   and climbed the wall
I climbed the wall   through a dim-lit corridor
The dim-lit corridor   leads to her empty sickroom
Her sickroom was empty   but the moon was full
The moon was full   the cicadas were crying
The cicadas were crying   *her unmade bed in the moonlight*
Her unmade bed in the moonlight   *an eternal stain*

I veered and turned   but couldn't find the exit
I couldn't find the exit   I said to my mother
I said to my mother   *the song is not over*
The song is not over   *you forgot to tutor me*
You forgot to tutor me   *the last secret phrases*
The last secret phrases   in my rented red Miata
In my rented red Miata   I veered and turned
I veered and turned   but couldn't find the exit

I couldn't find the exit   *the // rain // in // my // hair*

HOSPITAL IN OREGON

Shhh, my grandmother is sleeping,
They doped her up with morphine for her last hours.
Her eyes are black and vacant like a deer's.
She says she hears my grandfather calling.

A deerfly enters through a tear in the screen,
Must've escaped from those there sickly Douglas firs.
Flits from ankle to elbow, then lands on her ear.
Together, they listen to the ancient valley.

RHAPSODY IN PLAIN YELLOW

for my love, Charles (1938–2000)

Say: ䷒

I love you, I love you, I love you, no matter
   your race, your sex, your color. Say:
the world is round and the arctic is cold.
   Say: I shall kiss the rondure of your soul's
living marl. Say: he is beautiful,
   serenely beautiful, yet, only ephemerally so.
Say: Her Majesty combs her long black hair for hours.
   Say: O rainbows, in his eyes, rainbows.
Say: O frills and fronds, I know you
   Mr. Snail Consciousness,
O foot plodding the underside of leaves.
   Say: I am nothing without you, nothing,
Ms. Lookeast, Ms. Lookeast,
   without you, I am utterly empty.
Say: the small throat of sorrow.
   Say: China and France, China and France.
Say: Beauty and loss, the dross of centuries.
   Say: Nothing in their feudal antechamber
shall relinquish us of our beauty—
   Say: Mimosa—this is not a marriage song (epithalamion).
Say: when I was a young girl in Hong Kong
   a prince came on a horse, I believe it was piebald.
O dead prince   dead dead prince   who paid for my ardor.
   Say: O foot   O ague   O warbling oratorio . . .
Say: Darling, use "love" only as a transitive verb
   for the first forty years of your life.
Say: I have felt this before, it's soft, human.
   Say: my love is a fragile concertina.
Say: you always love them in the beginning,

then, you take them to slaughter.
O her coarse whispers   O her soft bangs.
  By their withers, they are emblazoned doppelgangers.
Say: beauty and terror, beauty and terror.
  Say: the house is filled with perfume,
dancing sonatinas and pungent flowers.
  Say: houses filled with combs   combs   combs
and the mistress' wan ankles.
  Say: embrace the An Lu Shan ascendency
and the fantastical diaspora of tears.
  Say: down blue margins
my inky love runs. Tearfully,
  tearfully, the pearl concubine runs.
There is a tear in his left eye—sadness or debris?
  Say: reverence to her, reverence to her.
Say: I am a very small boy, a very small boy,
  I am a teeny weeny little boy
who yearns to be punished.
  Say: I can't live without you
Head Mistress, Head Mistress,
  I am a little lamb, a consenting little lamb,
I am a sheep without his fold.
  Say: God does not exist and hell is other people—
and Mabel, can't we get out of this hotel?
  Say: Gregor Samsa—someone in Tuscaloosa
thinks you're *magnifico*, she will kiss
  your battered cheek, embrace your broken skull.
Is the apple half eaten or half whole?
  Suddenly, he moved within me, how do I know
That he is not death, in death there is

  certain // caesura.

Say: there is poetry in his body, poetry
  in his body, yes, say:

this dead love, this dead love,
  this dead, dead love, this lovely death,
this white percale, white of hell, of heavenly shale.
  Centerfolia . . . say: kiss her sweet lips.
Say: What rhymes with "flower":
  "bower," "shower," "power"?
I am that yellow girl, that famished yellow girl
  from the first world.
Say: I don't give a shit about nothing.
  'xcept my cat, your cock and poetry.
Say: a refuge between sleeping and dying.
  Say: to Maui   to Maui   to Maui
creeps in his pretty pompadour.
  Day to day, her milk of human kindness
ran dry; I shall die of jejune jejune   *la lune la lune.*
  Say: a beleaguered soldier, a find arse had he.
Say: I have seen the small men of my generation
  rabid, discrete, hysterical, lilliput, naked.
Say: Friday is okay; we'll have fish.
  Say: Friday is not okay; he shall die
of the measles near the bay.
  Say: Friday, just another savage
day until Saturday, the true Sabbath, when they shall
  finally stay. Say:
                    Sojourner
                              Truth.
Say: I am dismayed by your cloying promiscuousness
  and fawning attitude.
Say: *amaduofu, amaduofu.*
  Say: he put cumin and tarragon in his stew.
Say: he's the last wave of French Algerian Jews.
  He's a cousin of Helene Cixous, twice removed.
Say: he recites the lost autobiography of Camus.
  Say: I am a professor from the University of Stupidity,
I cashed my welfare check and felt good.

I saw your mama crossing the bridge of magpies
up on the faded hillock with the Lame Ox—
    Your father was conspicuously absent.
Admit that you loved your mother,
    that you killed your father to marry your mother.
Suddenly, my terrible childhood made sense.
    Say: beauty and truth, beauty and truth,
all ye need to know on earth all ye need to know.
    Say: I was boogying down, boogying down
Victoria Peak Way and a slip-of-a-boy climbed off his ox;
    he importuned me for a kiss, a tiny one
on his cankered lip.
    Say: O celebrator   O celebrant
of a blessed life, say:
    false   fleeting   hopes
Say: despair, despair, despair.
    Say: Chinawoman, I am a contradiction in terms:
I embody frugality and ecstasy.
    Friday Wong died on a Tuesday,
O how he loved his lambs.
    He was lost in their sheepfold.
Say: another mai tai before your death.
    Another measure   another murmur   before your last breath.
Another boyfriend, Italianesque.
    Say: Save. Exit.
Say: I am the sentence which shall at last elude her.
    Oh, the hell of heaven's girth, a low mound from here . . .
Say:
    Oh, a mother's vision of the emerald hills draws down her brows.
Say: A brush of jade, a jasper plow furrow.
    Say: ####00000xxxxx!!!!

Contemplate   thangs   cerebral   spiritual   open   stuff   reality
    by definition   lack   any   spatial   extension
we occupy   no space   and   are   not   measurable

we do not move   undulate   are not in   perpetual motion
where   for example   is thinking   in the head?   in my vulva?

whereas   in my female lack of penis?   Physical
thangs   spatial extensions   mathematically   measurable
preternaturally   possible   lack bestial   vegetable   consciousness
lack   happiness   lackluster   lack   *chutzpah*   lack   love

Say: A scentless camellia bush bloodied the afternoon.
    Fuck this line, can you really believe this?
When did I become the master of suburban bliss?
    With whose tongue were we born?
The language of the masters is the language of aggressors.
    We've studied their cadence carefully—
enrolled in a class to *improve our accent.*
    Meanwhile, they hover over, waiting for us to stumble . . .
to drop an article, mispronounce an R.
    Say: softly, softly, the silent gunboats glide.
O onerous sibilants, O onomatopoetic glibness.
    Say:
How could we write poetry in a time like this?
    A discipline that makes much ado about so little?
Willfully laconic, deceptively disguised as a love poem.

Say:
Your engorging dict-
atorial flesh
grazed mine.

Would you have loved me more if I were black?
    Would I have loved you more if you were white?
And you, relentless Sinophile,
    holding my long hair, my frayed dreams.

My turn to objectify you.
   I, the lunatic, the lover, the poet,
the face of an orphan static with flies,
   the scourge of the old world,
which reminds us—it ain't all randy dandy
   in the new kingdom.

Say   rebuke   descry

Hills and canyons, robbed by sun, leave us nothing.

FROM

HARD LOVE PROVINCE (2014)

ALBA: MOON CAMELLIA LOVER

for Don Lone Wolf

Last night through the camellia boles
I gazed, transfixed, at the moon—
Pale-faced, hook-nosed.
I know that she is my mother
Staring back from death, a dark matter.
For hours, we were one
With the earth's static blindness.
She did not envy the living
And I did not mourn the dead.
Tenderly, she lit up my face,
The camellia tree and my lover.
He, asleep on his side, cradling
His own soft sacks.

A few geese
Leave their noisy billows.
Home is a home away from home.
A neighbor's unfixed cat
Courting her own disaster.
A windless branch casts a hard silhouette
Certain of another tomorrow.

Suddenly, I witness the ecstasy of the changing hour—
As the sun devours the moon's corona
And the camellia unfurls
In brilliant pinks and red, and my new love,
With a sweet smile on his sour lips
Struggles toward the bathroom.
His flanks are glistening pearls.

O my mother,
Let the sunlight erase your final torso.
Let the milk of all suffering
Fade into the traffic's clean hum.
Let father's white suit of sin
Blanch into my lover's swooning moans
And all be forgiven.
Let my happiness blister and counter-glow
Against your magnificent   sick   light.

FORMOSAN ELEGY

for Charles

You have lived six decades   and you have lived none
You have loved many   and you have loved no one
You wedded three wives   but you lie in your cold bed alone
You sired four children   but they cannot forgive you

Knock at emptiness   a house without your love
Strike the pine box   no answer   all hollow
You planted plums near the gate   but they bear no fruit
You raised herbs in the veranda   fresh and savory

I cry for you   but no sound wells up in my throat
I sing for you   but my tears have dried in my gullet
Walk the old dog   give the budgies a cool bath
Cut a tender melon   let it bleed into memory

The robe you washed   hangs like a carcass flayed
The mug you loved   is stained with old coffee
Your toothbrush is silent   grease mums your comb
Something's lost   something's made strong

Around the corner   a new prince yearns to be loved
A fresh turn of phrase   a bad strophe erased
A random image   crafts itself into a poem
A sleepless Taipei night   a mosquito's symphony

Who will cry for you   me and your sister Colette
Who will cry for you   me and your Algerian sister
You were a rich man   but you held on to your poverty
You were a poor man   who loved gold over dignity

I sit near your body bag   and sing you a last song
I sit near your body bag   and chant your final sutra
What's our place on earth?   nada   nada   nada
What's our destiny?   war   grief   maggots   nada

Arms   cheeks   cock   femur   eyelids   nada
Cowl   ox   lamb   vellum   marrow   nada
Vulva   nada   semen   nada   ovum   nada
Eternity   nada   heaven   nada   void   nada

Birth and death   the same blackened womb
Birth and death   the same white body bag
Detach   detach   we enter the world alone
Detach   detach   we leave the world bone lonely

If we can't believe in God   we must believe in love
We must believe in love   we must believe in love
And they zip you up   in your white body bag
White body bag   white   white   body   bag

TWENTY-FIVE HAIKU

∎

A hundred red fire ants scouring, scouring the white peony

∎

Fallen plum blossoms return to the branch, you sleep, then harden again

∎

Cuttlefish in my palm stiffens with rigor mortis, boy toys can't love

∎

Neighbor's barn: grass mat, crickets, Blue Boy, trowel handle, dress soaked in mud

∎

Iron-headed mace, double-studded halberd slice into emptiness

∎

O fierce Oghuz, tie me to two wild elephants, tear me in half

∎

O my swarthy herder, two-humped bactrian, drive me the long distance

∎

Forceps, tongs, *bushi*, whip, flanks, scabbard, stirrup, goads, distaff, wither, awl

∎

Black-eyed Susan's, Queen Anne's lace, bounty of cyclamen, mown paths erupt

∎

Gaze at the charred hills, the woebegone kiosks, we are all God's hussies

I have not fondled the emperor's lapdog, whose name is Black Muzzle

Urge your horses into the mist-swilled Galilee, O sweet Bedlamite

Her Majesty's randying up the jewel stairs to find the pleasure dome

Ancient pond: the frog jumps in and in and in, the deep slap of water

The frog jumps into the ancient pond: she says, no, I am not ready

Coyote cooked his dead wife's vagina and fed it to his new wife

I plucked out three white pubic hairs and they turned into flying
monkeys

Let's do it on the antimacassar, on the antimacassar

Little Red drew her teeny pistol from her basket and said "eat me"

Chimera: Madame Pol Pot grafting a date tree onto a date tree

His unworthy appendage, his mutinous henchman grazed my pink
cheeks

He on top now changes to bottom, Goddess welcome her devotee

Fish fish fowl fowl, mock me Mistress Bean Curd, I am both duck and
  essence

Sing sing little yellow blight rage rage against the dying of the light

Don't touch him, bitch, we're engaged; and besides, he's wearing my
  nipple ring

BLACK PRESIDENT

If a black man could be president
Could a white man be his slave?
Could a sinner enter heaven
By uttering his name?

If the terminator is my governor
Could a cowboy be my king?
When shall the cavalry enter Deadwood
And save my prince?

An exo-cannibal eats her enemies
An indo-cannibal eats her friends
I'd rather starve myself silly
Than to make amends

Blood on the altar   Blood on the lamb
Blood in the chalice
Not symbolic   but fresh

ONE CHILD HAS BROWN EYES

One child has brown eyes, one has blue
One slanted, another rounded
One so nearsighted he stares internal
One had her extra epicanthic folds removed
One downcast, one couldn't be bothered
One roams the heavens for a perfect answer
One transfixed like a dead doe, a convex mirror
One shines double-edged like a poisoned dagger
Understand their vision, understand their blindness
Understand their vacuity, understand their mirth

STUDY HALL, DETERRITORIALIZED

for Gwendolyn Brooks

The brown boy hits me, but says he is sorry. The brown girl, his
sister, says it's because he likes me. I say, *yuk! He likes me? Well,
I hate him.* The black girl pinches me and says, *Scaredy-cat, tattletale,
little pussy, I dare you to hit back.* The white girl grabs my Hello
Kitty purse and spills my milk money. I karate-chop her arm.
The white boy says, *My father says that your father's egg rolls are made
of fried rat penises.* I answer, *Yep, my father says that the reason why
his egg rolls are made of fried rat penises is because Americans are weirdos
and like to eat fried rat penises.* The black girl laughs deep from her
gut and high-fives me. Just as I am redrawing the map, my little
fresh-off-the-boat cousin from Malaysia starts weeping into her
pink shawl like a baby, *wa wa wa.* The white girl muffles her ears,
Can't you shut her up?

I say, *Don't cry, little cousin, it's not as bad as it seems. It's verse!*
I point to the window and magically, to entertain us, two fat
pigeons appear cooing on the sill. The boy is sitting on top of the
girl, trying to molest her. She is wobbling, shuffling, pirouetting
under his weight. He is pecking a red, bald spot on her skinny
neck and singing:

> *We real cooooool   we real foooooools . . .*
> *We real cooooool   we real foooooools . . .*

Finally, we all laugh as one, laughing and laughing at God's
beloved creatures. Behind this spectacle, against all odds,
from the west, a strong explosion of sun bullies through the
big-gray-loogie-of-a-cloud.

SONNETNESE (AFTER SU TONG PO)

Ugly wives and bitchy concubines
they are one and the same

The blacker the black coffee   the more I want two cups
All I get in Beijing is shit Nescafé   sugary muck
Beauty / ugliness   selfsame skyline   obscured by smog
Imperial killjoy   drunk on his back   can't get it up
I love socialist architecture!   flabby husbands   alcoholic hard
      bucks
The sadder they get   the more I love them   I can't get
      enough
You could be a rich corpse   or a poor corpse
Stuff all your cavities   with jade and river pearls   powdery
      gold snuff
The robbers will pluck them   like fragrant florets
Silly boy   eyes closed   puckered   you wait for love
Gripe about how life has cheated you   of fame   of riches
End of a violent century   you are nostalgic for blood
My dear   we are staring at the void   at the edge of
      Americanness
The begonia is too beautiful   we must love   and be loved

SUMMER SLEEP (AFTER MENG HAORAN)

for Donald Justice

Summer sleep   I missed the dawn
My tired eyes   too heavy to open

Far off birds argue   freeways hiss
Car alarms trill   false emergencies

In dream I am ten   napping in the Master's house
My single bed   a one-girl coffin

Too tight! I cry   *my feet can't fit!*
He scowls and sighs   scorns my mediocrity

Rain dances   death coins on the roof
Time devours us   imperceptibly

Empty womb   pupils beg for entry
Unfinished poems   don't know how many

NOCTURNES

Beautiful moon   the murderer begins to sing
   The thief takes off his mask   to smell   the heliotrope

A dirty girl's face   against a clear night pane
   Dreams of a strawberry pie   at Marie Callender's

A junkie steals asters from a rich man's grave
   And spreads them   on the modest mound of his mother

A lone girl walks with moonlit haste   in the shadow of the
   maquiladoras

   ■

Pol Pot sleeps   counting heaven's lambs
   His ex-wife is learning Ikebana

The pine and the pagoda   so perfectly displaced
   She ponders the beauty   of the symmetrical

   ■

A pretty boy dances   naked in a cage
Twelve or thirteen   he is brown and slender
He sings   *My father sold me to the hillside wolves*
For a snort of the white dragon

   ■

Wild boar gnaws   on the boy's pretty face
   The boy gnaws   on pork tripe dumplings
Wild boar savors   the boy's rotting flesh
   The boy loves   his fragrant pork dumplings

The dead boy wades   face down in marl
    The dead boar's snout   points toward heaven
Lotus blooms   in the lord's cosmic soup
    To forgive   the eater and the eaten

■

The sky does not judge   it's black and starless
    The geese squawking high   plot their destination

The Goddess   sprawls   on a cool chaise lounge
    Feeds grapes   to her young paramour

■

The corpse of my love   reappears in a dream
    The corpse of my love   unzips his own body bag
His scarlet hand is turning brilliant green
    His purple heart   *tin   tin   na   bu   lations!*

■

A mask on horseback   is not your friend
    A mask on horseback   is not your savior

Run little sister beyond   the rabbit-proof fence
    As far as your skinny legs take you

■

Buddha cannot save you   he's detached   detached
    Christ hates himself   and other Jews in his image

No eternity   in the land you love
    Only eternal   the suffering

■

What is democracy   but too many things
    And too little time to love them

Cut up my body   rearrange my face
    Jackdaws   mole crickets   I am not afraid of you

        ▪

Every blossom   breaks my heart
    Every leaf falls   into memory

Every raindrop   cries on the shanty roof
    A streak of moonlight   blinds me

        ▪

The fat man of love is dead   Pavarotti and Barry White are dead
The fat man of love is dead   dead   dead!
Israel K   Alas!   Alas!

The fat man of love is dead   Elvis   dead   dead!
    Dead   dead   my maidenhead!

        ▪

The monkey claps and claps   his cymbals are tired
    Prosperity   decline   what does it matter?
    We will wind down this year   and slump over

        ▪

A deathblow is life blow to some
    Tell them   Emily   those wooly ministers

Chopin's fingers play   soft   soft   soft
    Comforting   the   beasts   and   flowers

EVERY WOMAN IS HER OWN CHIMERA

A suite for Adrienne Rich

Every woman is her own chimera
Today she is laughing with Julio
Tonight she is dancing with Coolio

■

How long can happiness last?
For a slow brief afternoon
My head on the thigh of a sequoia
Reading Wang Wei

■

Butterfly in mouth
　　But don't bite down
Whose life is it anyway?
　　She born of chrysalis and shit
Or she born of woman and pain?

■

Mei Ling brings a wounded poem
Crying　　*Please　Mommy　Mommy　　fix it!*
You wipe the tears from her cheeks
Then glue a gnat's torn wing

■

The sand dab flicks her tail
　　The tears of the wombat are green
Kiss me against the last hydrangea
　　Comrades we are not yet free

■

O sunlit *bourrée* of doves
      O moonlit cantata of red ribbon
Let's drum girls   let's ululate   let's praise
      The White-haired Maiden

    ▪

The Black Hawk scats   *vilip vilip vilip*
The Humvee murmurs   *surruu surruu*
Jackdaws boogie-down   *flip-flap flip-flap*
Marvin sighing   *mercy mercy mercy*

    ▪

All   I   want   is   love
My heart   my soul   my vulva
Yowl   *love love love*

    ▪

Look at him preen at the mirror
This aging retro-sexual
Combing combing his cowlick
In search of a perfect syllable

    ▪

Everybody's pregnant today
Even my cousin Louie
But cousin Louie is a man
Yes everybody's pregnant today
Even my cousin Louie

    ▪

Ax is chopping down Tree
Tree begs Ax to stop
Your handle is made of wood
We are born from the same mother

■

A pink horse is not a horse
A pink horse is not a horse
A pink horse is not a horse
A pink horse is not a horse

■

They will shave your head
Send you to the colonies
A brown man's musket
Will shoot you dead
He must defend his dignity

Do not do not believe in eternity

■

Poke me with an idle chopstick
I am mum as a flayed *ebi*
Bored with judgment and hate
And tired of pity

■

We must not be silenced
   Yet
      We   are
Silenced

Brush
      returning
to

      V O I D

■

It's not that you are rare
Nor are you extraordinary

O lone wren sobbing on the Bodhi tree
You are simple and sincere

BROWN GIRL MANIFESTO (TOO)

Metaphor   metaphor   my pestilential aesthetic
    A tsunami powers through   my mother's ruins
Delta   delta   moist loins of the republic
    Succumb to the low-lying succubus   do!

Flagpole   flagpole   my father's polemics
    A bouquet of   fuck-u-bastard flowers
Fist me   embrace me   with your phantom limbs
    Slay me   with your slumlord   panegyrics

Flip over   so I can see your pastoral mounts
    Your sword   slightly parting from the scabbard
Girl skulls   piled like fresh baked loaves
    A fowl wind   scours my mother's cadaver

Ornamental   Oriental   techno   impresarios
    I am your parlor rug   your chamber bauble
Love me   stone me   I am all yours
    Pound   Pound   my father's Ezra

Freedom   freedom   flageolet-tooting girls
Dancing   on the roof   of the *maquiladoras*

BEAUTIFUL BOYFRIEND

for Don Lone Wolf (1958–2011)

My skiff is made of spicewood   my oars are Cassia bract
Music flows   from bow to starboard
Early Mozart   cool side of Coltrane   and miles and miles
     of Miles
Cheap Californian Merlot   and my new boyfriend

    ■

My beautiful boyfriend   please shave your head
At the Miramar barbershop   take the tonsure
Bow toward the earth   prostrate and praise
Breathe in the Goddess's   potent citron

    ■

Bullet   don't shoot him   he's my draft-horse
Night scope don't pierce him   he's my love-stalk
Sniper   who are you   high on the roof
Stop for a slow cigarette   let him escape

    ■

If I could master   the nine doors of my body
And close my heart   to the cries of suffering
Perhaps   I could love you like no other
Float my mind   toward the other side of hate

    ■

The shantytowns of Tijuana   sing for you
The slums of Little Sudan   hold evening prayer
One dead brown boy is a tragedy
   Ten thousand is a statistic
So let's fuck   my love   until the dogs pass

All beautiful boyfriends are transitory
They have no souls   they're shiny brown flesh
Tomorrow they'll turn into   purple festering corpses
Fissured   gored   by myriad flies

My boyfriend drives up   in his late Humvee
Says: *We're going to   hunt bin Laden*
We'll sleep in caves   and roast wild hare
And rise to praise   the bright red sun

I was once   a beloved spotted ox
Now I've become   a war-horse of hate
I pulled the lorries   of ten thousand corpses
Before   I myself   was finally flayed

Down the Irrawaddy River   you lay yourself to sleep
No sun   no moon   no coming   no going
No causality   no personality
No hunger   no thirst

Skyward   beyond Angkor Wat
   Beyond   Jokhang Lhasa
You were floating   on a giant stupa
   Waiting   for   Our   Lord

Malarial deltas   typhoidal cays
Tsunamis don't judge   calamity grieves no one
The poor will be submerged   the rich won't be saved
Purge the innocent   sink the depraved

■

You push down my hand   with your bony hand
The fox-hair brush   lifts and bends
You sigh   *There's no revision in this life*
One bad stroke   and all is gone

■

What do I smell   but the perfume of transience
Crushed calyxes   rotting phloem
Let's write   pretty poems   pretty poems   pretty poems
Mask stale pogroms   with a sweet whiff of oblivion

QUIET THE DOG, TETHER THE PONY

Gaze   gaze   beyond the vermilion door
Leaf   leaf   tremble   fall
Stare blankly   at the road's   interminable end

Reduplications   cold   cold   mountains
Long   long   valleys   broad   broad   waters
Tears   are exhausted   now   shed   blood

Deep   deep   the baleful courtyards   who knows how deep
Folds on folds   of curtains
Gates   trap   infinite   twilight

Walk   walk   through   waning meadows
Steep   steep   toward   ten thousand Buddhas
Knuckles   blue   on the balustrade

In the land of   missing   pronouns
Sun   is a   continuous   performance
And we   my love   are   nothing

FOUR BUDDHIST TALES

From
REVENGE
OF THE
MOONCAKE
VIXEN (2009)

AFTER ENLIGHTENMENT,
THERE IS YAM GRUEL

When Buddha woke up hungry the animals offered him
their favorite food. The baby sea lion offered him day-old
fish bits that her mother regurgitated. The jackal offered a piece
of smelly rotting meat infested with maggots. The squirrel monkey
offered a handful of bruised bananas, veiled with gnats. The
hare was the most selfless of all. She went into the forest and
gathered an armload of wood, lit it on fire and placed herself in
the center as sacrifice. Mrs. Wong, exhausted from long hours
at the restaurant, was not impressed with the feast. She handed
Buddha a broom and said, "Old man, sweep the back porch first,
then the filthy hallway," and went to the kitchen and heated up
last night's yam gruel.

WHY MEN ARE DOGS

A long, long time ago in Hong Kong, a man and his dog
died side by side, both asphyxiated in a hotel fire. The
Goddess of Mercy, who happened to be jogging by with her
pedometer, decided to bring them back to life. She examined the
man's body and saw that this heart was shriveled and diseased by
smoking and bad eating habits, but the dog's heart was still in
good shape and was red, plump and healthy. She discarded the
man's diseased heart and replaced it with the dog's heart. For the
dog, she made a beautiful vegetarian heart with soy paste and
wheat gluten. She said some mumbo-jumbo New Age prayer and
the dog sprang up and wagged his tail and barked in gratitude.
The man, instead of thanking the Goddess, growled, scratched
his balls and tried to bite her head off for manifesting too late and
for not serving him steak tartar for dinner and not saving him
from the British Empire in the first place.

THE THEORY OF THE ONE HAND

The girlchild thrusts out her left hand.

The Great Matriarch says: *What if I cut it off, skewer it and sear it over briquettes for a Mongolian barbeque?*

The girlchild says: *Okay, Granny, weird, whatever you say.*

The Great Matriarch says: *What if I flay it like salmon sashimi, into fine thin pieces, display it on a large celadon plate with orange rind garnishes and feed it to your half-wit sister?*

The girlchild says: *Okay, Granny, gross, whatever!*

The Great Matriarch says: *What if I dice it with my scrap-iron cleaver and mix it up with ginger and scallions into a clear miso broth to feed the world's orphans?*

The girlchild says: *Okay, Granny, tee-hee, then that would be a benevolent, useful hand.*

The Great Matriarch says: *What if I grind it in a meat grinder, mixed with the ears of your illegitimate Japanese forefather, the entrails of your surfer-dude boyfriend, the clavicle of your Mexican ex-husband, the pancreas of your half-black hip-hop fuck-buddy in the afternoon and the tonsils of your half-green hippie fuck-buddy in the evening?*

The girlchild says: *Granny, stop spying on me! They're not fuck-buddies. They're just friends; well, friends with benefits . . .*

The girlchild says: *Tee hee. Okay, Granny, then let's call it "California Cuisine."*

The Great Matriarch says: *I am not joking, girlchild.*

The girlchild says: *But it's all very funny.*

The Great Matriach says: *No, it is not.*

LANTAU

While sitting prostrate before the ivory feet of the great
Buddha, I spilled almost an entire can of Diet Coke on
the floor. I quickly tried to mop up the mess with my long hair.
I peeked over my left shoulder: the short nun said nothing and
averted her eyes. To my right, the skinny old monk was consumed
by a frightful irritation of his own. He was at once swatting
and dodging two bombarding hornets that were fascinated
by his newly shaved head. "I hope he's not allergic," I whispered.
And beyond us was the motherless Asian sea, glittering with the
promise of eternity.

SELECTED
TRANSLATIONS

From MODERN CHINESE:
Ai Qing (1910–1996)

From NOM/VIETNAMESE:
Ho Xuan Huong (1772–1822)

From JAPANESE,
co-translated with the author:
Gozo Yoshimasu (1939–)

SNOW FALLS ON CHINA'S LAND

BY AI QING

Snow falls on China's land;
Cold blockades China.

Wind,
Like a grief-stricken old woman
Following close behind,
Stretching out her icy claws,
Tugs at the travelers' clothes.
With words as old as earth,
Her nagging never ends . . .

Coming from the forests
In horse-drawn carts,
You, there, farmers of China,
Wearing fur hats,
Braving the blizzard—
Where are you going?

I tell you, I too
Am a descendent of farmers.
From your faces etched with pain,
I understand deeply the years of labor
Of the men who make life on the prairie.

Yet I,
Floating on the river of time,
Am no happier than you.
Turbulent waves of hardship
Have so often swallowed me up,
Only to spew me forth.
In exile and in prisons, I have lost

The most precious days of my youth;
My life, like yours, is haggard.

Snow falls on China's land;
Cold blockades China.

On the river of this winter night,
One small oil lamp drifts slowly
In a rickety boat with a black sail.
Who sits there
In the lamplight, head bowed?

—Ah, it's you,
Tousle-haired and dirty-faced young woman!
Wasn't it your home,
That warm and happy nest
That was burnt down by the enemy?
Wasn't it on a night like this
When you lost your man's protection,
When in the terror of death,
You were teased and poked
By the enemy's bayonets?

On such cold nights as this
Our countless aged mothers
Huddle together in homes, not theirs.
Like strangers not knowing
Where tomorrow's wheels will take them.
And China's roads
Are so muddy, so rugged.

Snow falls on China's land;
Cold blockades China.

Passing over the fields in this snowy night,
Over regions gnawed by war's beacons,
Countless, the tillers of the soil
Who lost their livestock and homesteads,
Who lost their fertile farmlands,
Crowd together in life's hopeless squalor.
On this starving earth,
Gazing at the dark sky,
They reach out their trembling hands
And beg for succor.

Oh, the pain and misery of China,
As long and vast as this winter night.

Snow falls on China's land;
Cold blockades China.

China,
In this lampless night,
Can my feeble poem
Bring you a little warmth?

FROM UNTITLED EPIGRAMS (FOR OUR YOUTH)

BY AI QING

■

If you are afraid of storms at sea, you cannot be a soldier
If you are afraid of tigers, you cannot be a hunter

■

Selfishness with avarice breeds a snake
Of the deadliest venom

■

If you carry no weapon
You must not rush into the jungle

■

Who dares to shake the hand freshly stained by a comrade's blood?

■

Can you believe that when he raised his head high
He thought he was taller than the rest?

■

Those who lie without blushing
Will kill without blinking an eye

■

Cotton is afraid of fire
Tires are afraid of nails

■

The sea snail is an ingenious architect
His house is sturdy yet beautiful

Do not ask the beggar for alms
Do not ask the murderer for compassion

The kite is flying even higher
Escaping the child's grasp

Who can guess what is in the postman's bag—
How much joy, how much sorrow

Only the blossomed flower withers
Only the ripened fruit falls

When the holiday came, even the grass
At the foot of the wall is happy

The gate of the orchid garden is locked
Yet, it can't lock out the aroma

The flowers on the silk-kapok cloth are red and large
Yet there is not a trace of fragrance
The flowers of cassias and orchids are small
Yet their fragrance is very sweet

The most bashful flowers laugh loudly
Others bloom without sweetness

At dawn the old rubber tree smiles
As the cars roll by
Each tire says to her
"I was nurtured by your milk"

Is the wind chasing the waves
Or are the waves chasing the wind
Or are they leaping forward hand in hand?

The poet searches for the soul of the seagull
But the seagull is busy foraging for fish

As I was leaving the rostrum
A friend presented me two tangerines
—Silent applause

9 p.m.
The train enters the great Shanghai
My small son says
"We have come to the forest"

A lizard slithers over the grass
I ask a young girl from Shanghai
"What is that?"
She answers, "Bird!"

A,D,R,E,N,A,L,I,N

BY GOZO YOSHIMASU

Three o'clock, thirty-two minutes.
Mother Sun takes off her clothes at the entrance of summer.
Listen to the voice of the Spirit Diary: a righteous government
disappears. Cactus – midnight shower – a nude white body –
Mother Sun. Now, it is time for the first page of the Spirit Diary.

On the right corner of the Spirit Diary, a brook begins
from our southeast room. When you listen carefully, you can
hear a child's cry and a sweetheart's whisper . . . like
a cormorant that lost its nest. At the entrance of summer,
cries and murmurs ride the brook, flow into mysterious sound.

1976, June sixteenth, Land of Fire. We open the first page
to the northeast region. The Spirit's wheel turns
quietly. At the mouth of the river, I record the sounds that
will eventually disappear. I pray that someday a boy on
a bicycle will discover these sounds in a fossil.

I did not pass through hell
To you, Spirits, I send an immediate telegram
To drink milk
To memorize the names of flowers

The universe twists its lips. When a child cries in the
receptacle of night, I begin to walk on a path leading to
a shrine. I bid farewell to my first lover. The path
is a river of fire. The lover was the daughter of fire.

Reeds sing
za za za za za

A wind blows, through reeds, za za za za za. When they
utter, a boy with faith in the spirits hears the signals of
the universe, places a stethoscope on the noble woman's
chest and listens to her work. Echoes of ancient ballads
subside.

Over Birth Road, a swamp is a big house. A water oat, a
cut water oat, Mother Sun's lips are double vowels. I
listen carefully. I can listen quietly to the signals of
the universe and write poems. Za za za za za, placing a stethoscope
to an inlet of the swamp and to the noble woman, I take a shower.
There is a phone at the corner of my room, a brook that flows
beneath my legs.

Mother Sun, I am near a scandal. I am existing like a wet
river, water oat, a cut water oat. I write poems to tell
the real things: river for this, danger for that, lies for
this, sacrifices for that: and this, we call a white river bed.
To tell the real things, ignite fire, imagine a spiral pagoda, it
is a phantasmal runner.

I did not pass through hell
I will save that until after I die

To you, children of spirits, I send an immediate telegram
To drink milk
To memorize the names of flowers

Some day, I will return
That day, I will start fire

The brook whispers
Hu rrrr lll – a dice

The first page of the Spirit Diary. A pebble – hu rrrr lll,
the brook whispers, we begin the first step. The first page
is the riverbed of hell.

"The Minister of Foreign Affairs of Japan requests all those
whom it may concern to allow the bearer, a Japanese national,
to pass freely and without hindrance and, in case of need, to
afford him or her every possible aid and protection."

Thus
The river whispers

Then
Tokyo is a responsive transmitting station

We are children of cilium and reeds
Yes

Reed's children . . . Cilium's . . .
    Stethoscope and shower

Ahhhhh, the echoes of ancient ballads subside
    The subway's go-ro go-ro
    Ka-Ka, the coupling of trains

Machine's hip bones sews
    The curve around Suidobashi

From a medical office to a pharmacy
    An old woman walks
    Like a line of haiku
    On a path of fire
    To the stone tombs

Then
Tokyo is a responsive
    Transmitting station
    Oh children of reeds
    Send a telegram to the Minister of Japan

    Yearn for the post-war
    Korean pork barbeques

The brook whispers

> These are not words from the spiritual world. I do not own a
> membership card. Without a passport or ticket, I am all alone
> this summer day. At the entrance of summer I show my
> hand-made visa. Mother Sun proves her existence. This noble
> woman washes her hair, takes a shower, and floats her
> mysterious love. These are not words from the spiritual world.

From the medical office to the pharmacy
Adrenalin's
River
Is

Crossed
From a transmitting station to a receiving station

Prepare one boat, there is an insane person who will cross the
equinox   PREPARE ONE BOAT

Local post office to International Telegraph and Telephone:

Prepare a ferryman, give him his passport

    Inside the Spirit Diary, a nurse's mysterious voice sings out:

one drop of alcohol, surgical knife, adrenalin gauze. I am
afraid to breathe; my voice is filled with blood. Continue the
operation, alcohol, surgical knife, adrenalin gauze, adrenalin,
a, d, r, e, n, a, l, i, n.

Mother Sun. One o'clock, thirty minutes. Standing on a ferry
of the River of Fire, my ears cannot hear the phone. The river
whispers, trees start to burn, my lungs branch out.

Speaking in a voice that cannot be a voice causes screams

On the left corner of an era, catch a glimpse of the mysterious
brook's curve. That is the inlet. I make a raft, sew a soliloquy's
echo, scoop gravel with my hand. River within river,
the gangplank creaks under my feet.

One o'clock, fourteen minutes. Mother Sun is hairy. She is a
peeping silkworm sewing through a spirit's circuit. A larvae
walks through Birth Road, I hear its footsteps. Heart is a river
of fire, heart is fire's daughter. At the entrance of summer
Mother Sun takes off her clothes. At the moment of birth, with
all my strength and concentration, I look into the world.

I see a white shadow behind a sliding paper door.
I hear gasps, vibrations, clutching hair, cracking eggs

Uttering in a voice that is not a voice causes screams

At a quiet movie theater, I park my bicycle to look at the posters.
I bought a torn ticket from the lady at the window. Already I
hear the audience clapping.

Mother Sun rents out her house
Buys lemonade

Twice, thrice
I send a secret message

To you, Spirit's Children, I send an immediate telegram
I did not pass through hell
Please drink milk
And memorize the names of flowers

> 1976, June twenty-first. Land of Fire, back from the northeast,
> I open the first page of the Spirit Diary. I foresaw the Great Rock.
> The Great Rock reverberates. I walk on. An image of a woman
> appears from the rock. I walk on.
>
> Wind blows. Inside my brain the wind blows. I can see a tower
> of raging fire. My ears are the Spirit's ears. My eyes are
> the Great Pillars of Islam. My lips are wet in the Buddhist
> Way. Christ on the cross comes to me like the wind. I foresaw the
> Great Rock. A boy stands by its side, a round stage extending far
> back. Soon, the Great Rock starts to walk.

Man's shadow walks silently
        The face of a wall walks silently
The hall silently walks
        It is like a lake
The Great Rock takes a step with its left leg
        The boy lags behind
Joins hands with the rock
        walks the lake

> I feel an unfathomable deepness. For a moment, I completely
> lose myself. There is the Great Rock, there is the land of roots,
> there is the soft universe vibrating quietly. The world twists
> its lips. When a child cries in the receptacle of night, I begin
> to walk on Birth Road, bid farewell to my first lover.

I write a letter, and make a fair copy. I write a love letter,
wind and reeds. To the sound of the Great Rock's footsteps, I
write a love letter.

1976, August first, a window. The Spirit's Diary has many limbs
like the Asura. Hu rrrr lll – hu rrrr lll, somewhere the voice
of the train conductor calls out. O intense heat of August, am
I hearing an auditory hallucination?

A righteous government disappears. I listen to the premonition –
cactus, midnight, shower, a nude white body.

Last night, I passed through hell
To you, children of spirits, I send an immediate telegram
To drink milk
To memorize the names of flowers

This message is the last of the Spirit Diary. Children of summer,
did you write about the fine sky in your own diaries? I disappear,
leaving behind me a mysterious white cloud.

I did not pass through hell
But
I was born

Speech finished
Yours sincerely . . .

One drop of alcohol.

FIVE POEMS

BY HO XUAN HUONG

FLOATING SWEET DUMPLING

My body is powdery white and round
I sink and bob like a mountain in a pond
The hand that kneads me is hard and rough
You can't destroy my true red heart

JACKFRUIT

My body is like a jackfruit swinging on a tree
My skin is rough, my pulp is thick
Dear prince, if you want me pierce me upon your stick
Don't squeeze, I'll ooze and stain your hands

LAMENTING WIDOW

A woman wails, *boo hoo*, mourning her man
Shut up, shame on you, don't cry to the hills!
O little sister, I should have warned you
Don't eat the meat, if it makes you cough blood!

SNAIL

Mother and father gave birth to a snail
Night and day I crawl in smelly weeds
Dear prince, if you love me, unfasten my door
Stop, don't poke your finger up my tail!

WASPS

Where are you wandering to, little fools
Come, big sister will teach you how to write verse
Itchy little wasps sucking rotting flowers
Horny baby lambkins butting gaps in the fence

POETRY CAMP

A NEW PROSE POEM SEQUENCE (2015)

POETRY CAMP

Grandmother, when can I go to poetry camp?

What in the hell is poetry camp?

Where a bunch of teenage girls go into the woods to write poetry.

I know what teenage girls do in the woods and it's not poetry.

You may not go to poetry camp. You must scrub the soy sauce off the walls of the restaurant, then study for the SAT exam.

Grandmother, what if I spurn you and go to poetry camp?

Then you will shame your ancestors with your foolish dreams. And in your vain attempts to change your destiny, you will trip and fall off your platform shoes, break your neck and amount to nothing.

THANKSGIVING AT THE BREWSTERS

Dear Mei Ling:

We don't know how you became a self-righteous, left-wing vegan bigot so soon. At one week, you rejected mother's milk. At two months, you spat out a mouthful of congee that had a hint of sardine oil in it. At one year, you declared your independence from all flesh. At two, you broke your brother's nose for killing a cockroach, then invited an army of fire ants into your room and called them your sisters.

It's bad enough that we have to endure your bad habits daily, but must we be embarrassed in front of others as well?

We're used to your taking the shrimp out of the dumplings and eating only the skins. Picking off all the chicken pieces in the fried rice and feeding them to Mittens. But, we were shocked at your latest behavior (and mind you, we will report this to your developmental psychologist). Last Thursday at Grampy Brewster's you covered the turkey with your napkin and said it looked like a burnt Baby Jesus!

Then, you stripped naked to your nappies, raised your milk bottle, and swore to avenge the vanished Wampanoags. I hope you're satisfied now, young lady, for ruining a perfect family Thanksgiving!

Remember your holy-moly vegetarian auntie who lived near Vulture Peak and led a chaste life taking care of girl orphans?

Did she die of spiritual old age? No! She was hit by a bus during a peace rally in Lhasa and died of a brain hemorrhage.

DEAD BUDDHA

Dear Mei Ling:

We are sorry, but while you were away at Poetry Camp, we killed Buddha.

All night long he scratched around the back door, begging for food. He'd been gone for two weeks and came back all stinky and infested with ticks and field lice. You know how he is after a long fast. He prostrates himself and cries and cries! Who knows what he is crying about, as if all of humanity's weight were on his shoulders.

Unbeknownst to us, the little bastard begged at the Joneses first and had already chowed down leftover prime rib and bell pepper stuffed with mac & cheese. Mrs. Razo confessed to feeding him no fewer than four chicken enchiladas smothered with *mole poblano*. And Mrs. Ananda gave him okra lamb *Panang*, knowing full well that it was too spicy for his aged bowels. He's eighty in canine years, I reminded her, not a spring puppy.

Your brother fed him a giant heap of leftover garlic sesame pork: we were afraid that after four weeks stuffed to the back of the fridge the sesame oil went rancid; the carton was contaminated with vermin.

Please don't blame your brother. He stayed up deep into the night hunched over the linoleum, mopping up the bloody mess. At the break of dawn, he placed Buddha on his red wagon and pulled him to the rock garden. We chanted a few *ooooms*, then buried him next to Mittens II, in that quiet space between the wisdom pine and the twisted magnolia.

FIRST DUCK

Mei Ling, your absence at Poetry Camp occasions further news. A fat duck flew down to your plastic Hello Kitty play pool and stayed there quacking all week. I told your brother to drain the pool and shoo him away because we didn't want duck poop all over the place, but he refused to vanish and insisted that he speak to the Matriarch of the house—*that* being me.

When I went out to scold him, he bragged that he was a royal descendent, the 105th incarnation of the Great First Duck of the first Thanksgiving at Plymouth. He boasted that his ancestor was the first bird to be carved at the sumptuous high table and was enjoyed by the Great Chief Massasoit, his brilliant ambassador Squanto, and their Excellencies the Governor William Bradford and Captain Miles Standish . . . and therefore he may land on any damn standing or flowing pool of water in North America that he pleased! That we should be honored, he had graced us with his presence in this faded laughable plastic pee-stained cesspool we called existence.

Cesspool this! I shouted back. Forthwith, I grabbed him by his boastful scrawny neck and dragged him into the kitchen. I plucked his smelly feathers while listening to your brother practice the insufferable first bars of *Ode to Joy* on his piano over and over again for an hour. (Poor dear, he's really lousy. Maybe we should rent him a violin.) Then, I carved up his majesty in the famous Wong family free-style three-way aromatic duck.

First, I roasted him until his skin was dark brown and crispy, and flayed him perfectly so that the skin was paper thin: I served the first course as traditional Peking duck, with scallion spears, pancakes, and Hoisin sauce. Then, I sautéed the flesh in garlic and onions, half of which I diced with dried oysters and bamboo shoots and water chestnuts for lettuce cups . . . The other half I cut in strips with julienne carrots and wood ear presented with a vinegar sauce as a tangy warm salad. With the carcass, I made a delicious duck broth and froze two large cartons of it, to make your brother's favorite noodle soup later in the week.

Dutiful us, we have attached a before-and-after portrait of Prince Mr. Braggadocio Duck, posed, according to Feng Shui ritual, with his split bill pointing north and south on the celadon platter, garnished with some sprigs of green onion and four radish rosettes.

Please don't cringe at the finer details; we know that you are a freaky vegetarian.

While you stayed hiding out at Poetry Camp, Mei Ling, Grammy dreamt that a wild dog ran around our backyard with your left arm in his mouth. He ran in circles around the healing herb garden, then around and around the mung beans. From afar your arm shone like a prized catfish your Grampy once dragged up from the great Yellow River delta. Your arm thrashed and flapped around in his jaws. Your pretty jade bracelet made cracking sounds against his big teeth. The dog finally got tired and dropped the arm in front of me and fawningly said, "Mrs. Wong, I have heard about your culinary talents from far-away kingdoms. The grand master Lu Yu has dubbed you the Emeril Lagasse of Guangdong regional cooking. The connoisseur Liu Xie has said that he almost fainted whilst walking past your kitchen window, for the air was pungent with winter melon and aromatic mushrooms. Please simmer this arm with your famous black bean and garlic sauce. And I shall relish this like no other meal on earth."

Of course, Grammy refused his request and said, "Be off, evil spirit, I can't have a lousy, four-legged, dung mound reincarnation tell me how to serve up our precious girling! Black bean sauce is too vulgar! She deserves to be simmered in the richest manner, in five spice and the finest VSOP cognac! Be off, or I'll report you to the Ministry of Indentured Curs and Oxen." Cowering in defeat, he crawled backward in a respectful posture, eyes lowered, paws padding softly, and vanished into the ancient dogdom.

INDIGESTION

Dear Mei Ling:

For little girls with bad digestion, we suggest that you do not eat left-over noodles whilst reading the ancients or munch on nuked popcorn whilst watching trash TV. We further advise that you not lie on your back with your head pillowed under your smelly doggy, but that you lie on your right side, preferably next to a vial of fragrant lavender, and with your right arm crooked, propping up your head, imitating our beloved Sakyamuni in his last posture before entering Nirvana.

With your left hand—gently rub your belly, going clockwise, to release fire from the vitals. Perhaps sip some fresh ginger tea. By "fresh," we mean infused with generous slices from the true root brewed in the traditional slow method with honey or rock sugar and not the packaged fake stuff that you normally nuke from Trader Joe's.

If this doesn't work, swallow two spoonfuls of the pink ghee they call *Pepto-Bismol.*

DAO

NEW POEMS

DAO

When the superior girl poet meets the Dao
She glides her skateboard over it
Tries a 720 Gazelle Flip
Scrapes her elbow
Gets up, pivots
Nails an Ollie Impossible

Her dog Boo Boo and her cat Ssuma Chien
Watch in astonishment

When the inferior girl poet meets the Dao
She binges on ten back-to-back episodes
Of *Orange Is the New Black*
And postpones math

No consensus on what is Dao and what is not Dao
What is the way and what is impasse

Chaos said, "O, Mei Ling, give me eyes so that I can admire your beauty." So, Mei Ling punctured two wounds into his forehead. And as he gazed longingly into her eyes, Chaos said, "O, beautiful one, I can't smell your sweet scent." So, Mei Ling cut two holes for his nostrils. Chaos said, "O, melodious poet, give me two ears, so that I can hear your fine poems." Again, Mei Ling obliged. Chaos said, "At last, give me a sweet mouth, so that when we kiss my tongue could interlock with your tongue, deep into all eternity." And so, Mei Ling cut for him a deep red mouth and kissed it. Chaos said, "I have loved you too much" and bled from his seven sockets into turbulent rivers of blood, spilling over the dark continents, flooding the deforested plains and pestilential cities, destroying the once abundant border-lands. Finally, Chaos marveled at his own gruesome handiwork and would want for nothing.

SCARY POEM (INAUGURAL ETUDE, 2017)

Beware the tyrant's on the loose
Swinging his scythe and scrotum
Beware he enters your dreams
With a facemask and speculum
Beware he crawls on fours and sixes
Keeps time with the ancient pendulum
He's pissed as a newt
He chains you to his beliefs
Beware he will make you disappear
Your history will be rewritten
Beware, he sleeps in the same room
His smell is oddly human
Beware, he's a territorial beast
He'll carve you into twelve provinces
Beware, he flaunts his conquests
Beating his snare drum of flesh
Beware he is texting your sister
Whilst spraying his toxic gyzym
Beware he's ten thousand years old
And will survive the nexus pogroms
Beware he is the killer legacy
No muzzle nor museum can hold him

IMMIGRANT DREAM: EAT CROW

So, they lock you up in a two-and-a-half mat bamboo hut that they built with the help of Madame Mao. They shave off your long black mane and squeeze you into a cheapy too-tight faux mandarin frock and force you to eat crow. They mean, literally, eat crow. Most of your daddies are there—Trotsky, Marx, Beethoven, Bono, Sun Yat Sen and Richard Wright. They bring in stiff crow corpses, and in front of you they cook up crow into many revolting dishes: They chop up crow with a fast Ginsu knife as if chopping onion. They put whole birds into a meat grinder and make crow-burgers. They cube crow into little pieces and stir fry with cabbage. Crow chop-suey, crow lettuce cups, crow ala queen, crow souflee, crow-frappe, crow pate, crow tartar, stuffed buffalo crow-wings, and for dessert, they feed you lemon crow crumpets, flaming crow jubilee and crow tart à la mode. Just three dessert selections; they worry about your waistline.

And when you say: *No, Master-comrade, I have had enough. I'll lick your boot, I'll walk your poodle, I'll wash your car, stop, stop! I am a non-denominational Daoist Vegan. I hate crow!*— they cackle and force-feed you more crow. The final straw is that when your little Buddhist granny taxis over with your favorite after-school treat, they do a switcheroo and replace her Tupperware of savory chive dumplings with crow bars!

You eat so much crow that the crow society has penned a letter to the Minister of Injustice that says enough is enough, you are decimating our people to make a point!

LITTLE BOX OPENS UP

■

Little Box talks back
With a new set of teeth
And pink gums
A fake nose and a wax mustache
She disguises her voice
To sound like Groucho

■

Little Box opens up
And cries to her psychiatrist
I don't know why they hate me
I'm such a sweetheart
I volunteer at the zoo
And teach Mandarin
To their bratty children

■

Little Box is not happy to see you
So, she closes shop for months
Years, decades and two millennia!
She tacks up a sign that says
Nirvana

■

Little Box is undead
She sleeps all day in a coffin
Hands over chest
At night she cruises the mall
For juicy victims

She prefers type A
But AB if she has to
What can you say
Vampires can't be choosy
She likes your stupid brother

■

Little Box is on the psychiatry couch
Everybody hates me
Nobody loves me
Little Box lies on her side
And spills her guts

■

What's in Little Box
A perfect orchid
A chocolate covered strawberry
A new iPhone
With a glittery sleeve
Amber earrings from Pushkin

Keys to a new Porsche
A retro Chanel brooch
A Getty scion's left ear
A czar's penis
Gifts so rare
Please don't stare

■

What's in Little Box
Rancid chow mein
A sliver of cold pizza
Last week's hummus

You're a starving orphan
From East Brooklyn
And you'll eat it

■

So, you want to fuck Little Box
You want to know her secret
She won't open up
She won't give it up
And you are genuinely repelled
By her filthy ribbon

■

You want to DO the Little Box
You are a sorry story
You big creep
Why don't you get off the couch and find
A real girlfriend!

■

Boss Box
White, square and without a soul!

■

Please don't analyze Little Box
She's just cardboard clogging the landfill
Her mother Precious Jade Purse
Has been re-gifted

BAMBOO, THE DANCE

How free and lush the bamboo grows, the bamboo grows and grows
Shoots and morasses, fillies and lassies and shreds and beds and rows
O phloem and pistil, nodes and ovules
    The bamboo grows and grows
Her release, her joy, her oil, her toil, her moxie, her terror, her swirl
Dig deeper into soil, deeper into her soul, what do you find in my girl
Thrash of black hair and silken snare, face in the bottom of the world
Bound by ankles, poor deer, poor sow, O delicate hooves and fascicles
    Dead doe, dead doe, dead doe
Wrists together, searing red tethers, blood draining from her soles
    O choir, O psalm, O soaring fearsome tabernacle
The bamboo grows, the bamboo grows and grows
Through antlers and eyeholes, O sweet soul, O sweet, sweet soul

Thin green tails, purple entrails, the bamboo grows and grows
She flailed and wailed through flimsy veils, through bones and
    hissing marrow
Nobody to hear her, but wind and chaff, a gasp, then letting go
They loved her, then stoned her, buried her near her ancestors
    My mother, my sister, my soul

Shimmering mesh, a brocade sash, hanging on a distant oracle
Springboks dance on shallow mounds, echoes, echoes, echoes

FOR MITSUYE YAMADA ON HER 90TH BIRTHDAY

They say we bitch revolutionaries never go out of fashion
Wearing floppy hats and huge wedgy shoes
A feather bandolera and a lethal python

Sometimes we wear a fro-perm cause we hate our straight hair
Sometimes we wear it straight to the ankles like Murasaki

I bleached mine purple to look like Kwannon Psylocke
Maxine's beaming, like the Goddess of Nainai temple
A cross between Storm, the X-girl and Ahsoka Tano

We love our laser eyes, our Yoko granny glasses are dizzy!
Short women poets unite! Revolution ain't just style
It's destiny!

■

We will make a comeback, we always do
You and Nellie and Meryl making a rad film
Janice in a miniskirt testifying at Glide Church
Hisaye still svelte with her bluesy magpie clarinet
Wakako dancing to a Taiko drum and Sheila E
Rats! The FBI's rifling through your garbage again
Bastards are after your studded bellbottoms and a *raison d'etre!*

Boys, you can have them, even my embroidered hot pants!
We'll drag it with Cher, sporting black bangs of resistance
We'll emolliate our bras at the Atlantic City Boardwalk
Listening to Buffy Saint Marie and fusionist Jazz bash
Angela Davis and Che, spinning revolution in our brain
When an album was a symphony
Not a blip on a Spotify Lumumba
We'll lip-sync to Marvin Gaye and mash to Soul Train

And stage a sing-along-sit-in with Odetta!
Forget about Dylan, he's a whiner
Where's Jamie Baldwin, where's Dick Gregory?
Soak our gall with bell hooks and Barbara Christian
O sweet Jesus! Allen G's chasing your nephew around the Bodega

Imagine the long march with Mao or MLK or Harvey Milk
Study the physiognomy of foreheads and twisted fate
I was a naïve girl-poet wearing wet nappies
While you were fighting the WRA
And Executive Order 9066

Where is Manzanar, where is Topaz, where is Tule Lake?
Wherefore, Gila River and Heart Mountain?
Sound like vacation hotbeds
Where rich white retirees play bingo and waltz!

They whisked your father away deep into the night
Auctioned your house off to some sleazy Hollywood exec

Hell, nobody knew
We were suckling on the tithes of the early Renaissance

Drove a pink Buick to a poetry camp called Woodstock
Ate hashish with Sylvia Plath's ghost at an Irvine bus stop
Binged on Neruda's psilocybin odes at Bullfrog

(Meanwhile, let's mock a Whitmanesque praise poem at the Iowa
    Workshop)
They say don't write political, girl, just hang yourself with abjection!

Let's bum rush a haiku party with conceptual artists
How long can you stare at a urinal, for god's sake!

What's the difference between the old regime and the new regime?

The new one has lite sabers and a bona fide Wookiee

I confess, I was faking it, I was a revolutionary freak!
Did a hunger strike with Cesar Chavez cause he's sexy
Mao was a new crush, Marx whetted the yoni,
I was just a horny girl-poet, please forgive me

I binged on duck noodles on Clement Street after sucking down a bong
Wrote ten thousand letters for Amnesty International high on schrooms

But I confess that on the second day of a relapse
I threw up alphabet soup all over my slutty girlfriend's Austin Healy
She thought she was a dikey James Bond, oh really!
I lied that the dog did it!

    For your 90th birthday, my dear Auntie Mitsuye
    I write you this silly poem
    not counting syllables, accentuals or diphthongs
    not making it sing or pulling a long conceit
    out of a colonialist's ass-
    anine simulacra, or trying to rap with the youngsters
    wearing a Compton cap.   Or break-dancing
    for an endstop
    Jeremaiad

    Not trying to make a hybridity lipidity sonnet
    the volta is loving   my vulva   lapping vodka   on the Volga!
    not a long religious rant about a pussy Jeoffry,
    nor dogging the dogma dharma
    who left her yellow mark all over the doggity diaspora
    not lifting a hind leg   but squatting in the morning glory
    like a real Asian Diva

They paid you
20,000 for your civil liberties

A mule and ten acres of scorched paddy apotheosis

They slapped a cruel judgment on the new century
There will always be another brown girl to hate
Rape her village, burn her wedding veil, shoot her in the face
Plant a black flag on her sweet soul
Strap her down with a ticking heart-bomb and show no mercy

Auntie Mitsuye
No more redress, no more reparations, no worries about legacy
Let's live raunchily and have the last laugh

Somewhere in a faraway kingdom
We shall eat that magical pill of immortality

You and me and Emily D.
Gnawing ganja cookies, dreaming on our backs
And Bessie's crooning her heart out on a crappy 8-track!

POSTSCRIPT:
BROWN GIRL MANIFESTO, ONE OF MANY (2010)

I. A performative utterance: each utterance of the first-person "I" as the speaking subject combats the history of oppression which extends to me. Through the spoken word, the "I" critiques, questions, corrects, annotates, examines, mocks, derides, offends, and talks back at the prevailing culture.

When I perform my poetry, the "I" speaks not only as the "poet" but also through enacted "difference"—through a body inscribed by historical determinations: brown (dirty), immigrant (illegal alien), girl (unwanted, illegitimate). An "I" as the brown-girl body who faces her audience stands there vulnerable to the perennial history of pre/mis-conceptions, racism, and hatred. (If we think that the brown-girl figure is no longer viewed by historical determinations, then we are in denial of our role in her existence in the global situation.)

II. Who is this "I" that is not "I"? The sex that is not One. She who is not allowed to speak. Like the old world feminist that I am (who represents something larger than myself—why should I not have ambitions for an art that is political?), should I not want to speak on behalf of the marked brown-girl:

the veiled "subaltern" from the (un) "Holy Lands"? the girl who is burned for a better dowry? the 24-year-old undocumented worker whom you both need and despise who died in the desert south of Dateland, Arizona traveling across the border? the nameless girl among thousands toiling in the factories in Guangdong? a nameless girl murdered near the maquiladoras in Juarez? The perennial girl orphan, starving, crying, pushed from refugee camp to refugee camp? From Kauma, to Za' atari to Vida . . . The most annoying of all, she is also your immigrant neighbor, the one with the screaming baby on her hip; the one you despise most of all, because her very existence, her moving into the neighborhood, has brought down the value of the real estate.

III. The speaking subject is always an oppositional voice. If the majority says "no dogs allowed," she says "grrr" and wags her tail and bites the man in the ass and won't let go. If the majority says, "we don't want you, immigrant, we'll send you back," the speaking subject writes on the walls of Angel Island, "I shall stay firm, I shall endure; I shall not be erased."

IV. Artistic subjectivity: the "I" authorizes first-person subjectivity and enables artistic expression, which differs from autobiography. A brown-girl subject is not necessarily for sociological or ethnographical inquiry.

My grandmother is in the kitchen making dumplings. Yum, you say, what are the ancient ingredients – better yet, what ancient rites are you conducting? Don't you perform ancient rites in the kitchen? – let me bring my notepad, and my camcorder – this is important research (I'll get tenure). But wait a minute, this is poetry. My grandmother is in the kitchen making dumplings out of General Iwane Matsui's liver, and we have entered the realm of magical realism.

Perhaps you better not stay in that kitchen and get the hell outta there!

Why should Maxine's "cutting the frenum" be forever subjected to the litmus test of an "authentic" autobiographical (ethnographical) experience when even Gregor Samsa gets to speak? Why is a cockroach a speaking subject (laconic, nonetheless, decrying "mother, mother")? The ethnographers never question whether or not he is a descendent of other cockroaches. But seriously, why should you get to imagine yourself as Luke Skywalker and I can't imagine myself as the Woman Warrior? Aren't Chinese American girls allowed to have a surreal imagination?

V. The speaking subject is also the lyric poet: am I making art or am I only producing material for your ethnographical interest? Am I not also spewing out sonnets, palindromes, epigrams, rondeaus, haiku, renku, ballades, jueju, fu, ghazals, prophetic hallucinations and all the sweet and wild brilliant interstitial variations of the above? Am I not the poet of witness? Am I not a disciple of Nellie Sachs and Paul Celan trying to describe the horrors of the Holocaust, meanwhile inventing a new lyric, which questions the possibility/impossibility of poetry after the most heinous episodes of history? Am I not a descendent of Qu Yuan, whose lyric intensity caused him to drown himself in the Mi Lo River in protest? And the descendent of the courageous feminist poet Qiu Jin, who recited a poem on the path to her own beheading?

VI. A Call for Unity. Brothers and sisters of the revolution: contemplate for a moment, are we really now in a post-identity, post-racial, post-feminist era—and all is groovy and color blind—equal work, equal pay, equal justice for all? We are in the first term of the first black presidency in the U.S.A. Are we therefore all emancipated and free? Do we all have a stake in the American dream? Do we all have a place at the table (or do we still have to cook it for you, serve it and wipe the floor after you too, and sit quietly in the dark kitchen while you delight in that lush banquet)?

Why am I still standing here trying to answer to you: hegemonic economy, mordant philosophers! poebiz mongers! treacherous cognoscenti! cultural flesh-traders, fascist (es)states! trickster patriarchs! pallid leaseholders, cleaver-wielding grandmothers! erstwhile dreamers, readers, overlords: yeah you, you are never satisfied!

PEONY APOCALYPSE

Why must I tell you this story, O little one
You're just a bud-of-a-girl, who knows nothing

Now you are full-faced, bright as sun
Now you open your skirts pink, layered, brazen

Suffering is alchemy, change is God
Now you droop your head, heavy with rust

Sit, contemplate, what did Buddha say?
Old age, sickness, death, no one owns eternity

Detach, detach, look away from the sun
Let your petals fall aimlessly

Don't despair, little one, we are done

NOTES

PREFACE

"Summing up" and "retrospective" are words that Adrienne Rich used in her foreword in *Poems: Selected and New, 1950–1974*.

DWARF BAMBOO

"The Cricket." Yang Guifei (719–756) was the beautiful concubine of the Tang dynasty emperor Xuanzong. She was blamed for the downfall of the empire and was executed by the emperor's army. Cixi (1835–1908) was the notorious empress dowager who also began her rise as an imperial concubine and ruled the Qing dynasty for forty-seven years. She, too, was held responsible for the downfall of the kingdom.

"We Are Americans Now, We Live in the Tundra." Ling Ling and Xing Xing are two giant pandas China presented to the United States as a goodwill gesture following Nixon's visit to the People's Republic of China in 1972.

"Ode to Anger." *Dim mak* are deadly pressure points along the meridians of the body. In Kung Fu combat, a master could attack these tender points, thus causing immediate or delayed death. It was rumored that Bruce Lee died from having received a secret blow to his *dim mak*.

"Love Poem from Nagasaki." Response poem to the film *Hiroshima Mon Amour*. Hiroshima and Nagasaki, two Japanese cities, were atom-bomb targets.

THE PHOENIX GONE, THE TERRACE EMPTY

The title refers to a line in Li Bai's famous poem, "登金陵鳳凰臺"

"A Portrait of the Self as Nation." I wrote this poem in response to the first President Bush's "gulf war." It turned out to be a prescient poem that augured a second Bush war. *Jing Pingmei* refers to a Chinese erotic novel. "Exclusion" refers to various "exclusion acts," anti-Chinese legislation that attempted to halt the flow of Chinese immigrants to the United

States. "Hookworm" and "trachoma" are diseases that kept many Chinese detained and quarantined at Angel Island. "Hibakushas" are scarred survivors of the atom bomb and their affected descendants. "Babylonia" refers to the ancient land that is now part of Iraq.

RHAPSODY IN PLAIN YELLOW

"That Half Is Almost Gone." 愛 is the Chinese character for love: The semantic radical for the character of love is 心, which is a pictograph for the heart. "Ai, ai" is an exclamation homophonous with "ai," the word for love, punning love with pain.

"The Colonial Language Is English." "The Dao of which we speak is not the eternal Dao. The name that we utter is not the eternal name" comes from Laozi.

"Take a Left at the Waters of Samsara." Samsara is the Hindu and Buddhist continuous cycle of birth, death, and rebirth. This chain of eternal suffering is a result of karma, accumulated debts from evil and sinful actions.

"Chinese Quatrains (the Woman in Tomb 44)." These individual quatrains are adapted from jueju, literally "cut verse," four lined poems, usually five or seven characters per line. I have mixed Chinese and Western quatrains into a form I call "Chinese-American quatrains," in which each quatrain is self-contained and yet are linked together in a sequence like stunning pearls in a necklace. Of course, the sum should be even more impactful than the parts.

"Cauldron." The poem is shaped like a myriad of three-legged bronze ceremonial cauldrons (*ding*), one piled on top of another. The final shape should look like one large, abstracted cauldron. Yuan Shikai (1859–1916) was a famous warlord who tried to seat himself as emperor in the tumultuous Qing dynasty. 亂 is the Chinese and Japanese Kanji character for *chaos*. It is also the title for Kurasawa's famous film *Ran*. In the opening scene, a warrior rides his warhorse in the shape of this pictograph.

"Variations on an Ancient Theme: The Drunken Husband." The dog barking is a conventional image in many Chinese poems. The drunken husband is also a conventional character. In the classic tale, the woman pines all night for her man, then receives him gratefully as he comes home drunk, having been carousing all night in a brothel. My remake gives this tale a contemporary turn about domestic violence.

"Bold Beauty." Cai Yen was the wife of an important official in the Later Han dynasty. During the Tatar invasion, she was captured and served as consort to the Tatar chieftain for twelve years. She was finally ransomed and returned to her family. However, she was forced to leave her sons behind. She wrote very moving poems about her experience in captivity and is hailed as one of the most important women poets in Chinese history.

"The True Story of Mortar and Pestle." This tale is a "reinvention" of a classical Chinese ghost story.

"Tonight While the Stars Are Shimmering." "Between heaven and earth, a pesky brown gull" is a line from a Du Fu poem. The brown gull represents the poet. "Prayer mat" refers to a classic Chinese pornographic novel, "The Prayermat of Flesh."

"Get Rid of the X." This poem is a "reinvention" of a famous poem by the Tang poet Li Bai, "Drinking with the Moon."

"Identity Poem (#99)." *Poidog* is American-Hawaiian slang for a mongrel, a mixed-race person.

"Rhapsody in Plain Yellow." This long title poem began as a twenty-page collage rant with over fifty puns, riddles, and allusions. I managed to cut it down to six pages. Here are a few explanations of various allusions.

"Rhapsody" mocks the Chinese *fu* form, originally characterized by ornate rhymed prose couplets and exposition. The title also alludes to Gershwin's "Rhapsody in Blue." Therefore, I am a Chinese-American poet inspired by a Jewish-American composer who borrows from an African-American blues tradition but writes in a high European symphonic tradition.

"An Lu Shan" is a famous rebel warrior who tried to topple the kingdom during the Tang dynasty. "Combs, combs" refers to a haiku by Buson (1716–1783): "The chilling feel / my dead wife's comb / under my heel."

"God does not exist . . . hell is other people" refers to Sartre's famous lines.

"Friday Wong" refers to the character "Friday" in Daniel Defoe's *Robinson Crusoe*.

"To Maui, to Maui, to Maui" mocks Macbeth's monologue "Tomorrow, and tomorrow, and tomorrow," a shout-out to both my friends in Maui and to Shakespeare.

HARD LOVE PROVINCE

"Alba: Moon Camellia Lover." According to Chinese folklore, one should be able to see one's lover's face in the full moon. This poem subverts the Chinese poetic tradition as the speaker sees her dead mother's profile in the moon, instead, while she is in bed with her lover.

"Formosan Elegy." Throughout my books, I play with jueju, Chinese-American "cut-verse" quatrains. Some variations sound more like English folk ballads, while others are inspired by Emily Dickinson's fractured hymns. Each quatrain is self-contained, very much in the Chinese fashion, and in a sequence the quatrains work sometimes in harmony but often as oppositional forces. There are various sequences throughout the book that echo each other in theme. Some recurring images and refrains loosely tie the book together, creating both dissonance and harmony. I call this piece an elegiac Chinese-American ballad. The elegy begins in the Western narrative tradition. But it then unravels into a jazzy improvisational zen funereal mantra toward the end. "Nada Brahma" refers to the concept that the world is energy and sound. "White body bag": white is the funereal color for Buddhists, not black. "Ilha Formosa" means "beautiful island." *Formosa* is the Colonial Portuguese name for Taiwan.

"Twenty-Five Haiku." In the original Japanese form, the haiku is written in one long vertical line and not broken up into three-lined verses. I played with different caesura patterns in these twenty-five variations, transgressing the five-seven-five traditional pauses in the English haiku tradition. Yes, the two frog haiku refer to the famous Basho haiku, however "subverted" or "perverted."

The famous "frog" poem by Basho.
In Kanji:
古池や蛙飛こむ水のおと
In Hiragana:

ふるいけやかはづとびこむみづのおと
In Romaji:
Furuike ya kawazu tobikomu mizu no oto

"One Child Has Brown Eyes." An epicanthic fold refers to the skin fold of the upper eyelid, covering the inner corner of the eye, mostly seen in people of "Asian descent."

Many starlets change the shape of their eyelids, making "round eyes" that conform to Western notions of beauty.

"Study Hall, Deterritorialized." This *haibun*, a Japanese prose poem form punctuated by a fit of verse, is set in a "multicultural" Californian classroom that I visited in San Jose. The kids were lively, to say the least. I couldn't tell if they were talking or fighting. Instead of punctuating the *haibun* with a haiku, I commemorate Gwendolyn Brooks's iconic poem "We Real Cool."

"Sonnetnese." I love the sonnet and have experimented with many "free" sonnets that merge with Chinese themes and references. This one is fashioned after Su Dongpo's famous poem—I wrote the first draft in Beijing after visiting Mao's corpse at his mausoleum.

"Summer Sleep." One summer, I tried to visit my old teacher, Donald Justice, but he was very ill and couldn't receive me. I wrote this poem for him. I love the Chinese tradition of writing poems for friends and honoring one's teachers with a poem. It is also inspired by a famous poem by the great Tang dynasty poet Meng Haoran.

春眠不覺曉
處處聞啼鳥
夜來風雨聲
花落知多少

Word-for-word trot:

Spring Dawn by Meng Haoran

    Spring sleep not wake dawn
    Place place hear cry bird
    Night come wind rain sound
    Flower fall know how many

"Every Woman Is her Own Chimera." This is another quatrain sequence with a lot of scatting and jazzy improv.

"A Pink Horse Is Not a Horse" is riffing off a famous Chinese conundrum in the *White Horse Dialogue* (白馬 論;), attributed to the philosopher Gongsun Long (325–250 B.C.), Gonsun Long (n.d.) in Wikipedia. Retrieved November 21, 2017. Wikipedia.org/https://en.wikipedia.org/wiki/Gongsun_Long.

One interlocutor (sometimes called the "sophist") defends the truth of the statement "A white horse is not a horse," while the other interlocutor (sometimes called the "objector") disputes the truth of this statement. This has been interpreted in various ways. Possibly the simplest interpretation is to see it as based on a confusion of class and identity. The argument, by this interpretation, plays on an ambiguity in Chinese. The expression "X is not Y" (X非Y) can mean either:

"X is not a member (or subset) of set Y"

"X is not identical to Y"

Of course, a "pink horse" has its own wild ramifications. The conundrum interrupted by a girl!

"Quiet the Dog, Tether the Pony." I originally sketched out the first four stanzas in rough classical Chinese in my notebook. Then I translated the poem into English. I tried to avoid using pronouns, but I couldn't help using "we" in the last triplet.

TRANSLATIONS

Ai Qing (1910–1996)

"Snow Falls on China's Land"

Ai Qing, one of the most important and beloved revolutionary poets in modern China, wrote the iconic poem "Snow Falls on China's Land" in the winter of 1937, during the Sino-Japanese War. The poem became a revolutionary anthem, and even today children know its refrain by heart. He wrote this poem in simple vernacular Chinese, in accessible language that everyone could understand. Indeed, he helped Chinese poets emerge from the classical era of ancient airs and ponderous allusions. Classical Chinese poetry had lost its relevance by the nineteenth century. Ai Qing's poems highlighted the suffering of ordinary people in wartime and feudal poverty. He was truly a poet "of the people."

In 1958, Ai Qing was purged in the Communist "anti-rightist" campaign and exiled to Sinjiang Uygur Province for almost two decades. All the poems he wrote during this era are lost. After his "rehabilitation" in 1975, in the last years of his life, he returned to Beijing as a lionized national treasure.

"From Untitled Epigraphs"
Ai Qing wrote a variety of travel poems, aphorisms, and folk tales in the volumes published after his "rehabilitation." I interviewed him when he visited the International Writing Program at the University of Iowa in 1979. He said that he wrote these simple pieces for "the youth of China."

Gozo Yoshimasu (1939–present)

Gozo Yoshimasu is one of the most important avant-garde artists living in Japan. He is a multimedia literary artist whose innovative poetry transcends the page in groundbreaking ways, often mixing texts with elements of performance, photographic, and video art. It is almost impossible to categorize his vast and brilliant work.

I met Gozo at the International Writing Program at the University of Iowa in 1979, where he performed his poems against the background of a haunting Japanese flute. As we worked together translating "*A,d,r,e,n,a,l,i,n*," I tried to catch the incantatory essence of his voice and also to capture both the ancient and the contemporary spirit of postindustral Japan.

Ho Xuan Huong (1772–1822)

Ho Xuan Huong is considered "the Queen of Vietnamese Nom poetry" (Poetry Foundation). Her father was a scholar and her mother a high-ranking concubine. She herself became the concubine of two minor officials. In her poetry, Huong wrote fervently about women's issues. Her poems railed against Confucian hierarchical order and polygamy; they lampooned the profligate generals and the Buddhist clergy alike. She employed brilliant wit and blatant double entendre, creating unforgettable subversive erotic images.

POETRY CAMP: A NEW PROSE POEM SEQUENCE

"Thanksgiving at the Brewsters." Grampy refers to the Elder William Brewster (1611–1650), the first religious leader of the pilgrims at the Plymouth Colony. "Wampanoags" refer to a Massachusetts tribe that was decimated by smallpox.

"Dead Buddha." Buddha died after having eaten tainted pork. He could not refuse food from the people, even if it was rancid.

"Dogdom." Lu Yu: Song dynasty poet and connoisseur of gastronomy and tea. Liu Xie: first famous literary critic in China; he lived in the fifth century.

DAO, NEW POEMS

"Bamboo, the Dance" was written for the Terezin Music Foundation for the 70th anniversary of the liberation of Nazi concentration camps. The "dead doe" image comes from a folk song in the *Shijing* (Book of Odes), the oldest anthology of Chinese poetry, dating around 1100–600 B.C.

"For Mitsuye Yamada on Her 90th Birthday" was finally finished two years after Mitsuye's celebration party. "Executive Order 9066" was signed by Franklin Roosevelt on February 19, 1942, which ordered the removal of Japanese Americans from their homes to be incarcerated in various military internment camps in the west.

 "Topaz," "Tule Lake," "Gila River," "Heart Mountain" are all names of internment camps.

 Nellie Wong, Meryl Woo, Maxine Hong Kingston, Wakako Yamaguchi, Janice Mirikitani, and Hisaye Yamamoto are all activist writers of Mitsuye's generation.

 There are too many '60s, '70s, and contemporary references to discuss here. I included such elaborate references to serve as a myriad "memory gift" to help Mitsuye celebrate her 90th birthday.

"Brown Girl Manifesto, One of Many" was inspired by Mina Loy's "Feminist Manifesto" and June Jordan's "A Poem About my Rights," and was first written as a performance monologue and was performed at the Iowa Workshop 75th anniversary celebration.

 Of course, it was totally inappropriate for the occasion.

INDEX